NATIONALISM
Political Cultures in Europe and America, 1775–1865

Studies in Intellectual and Cultural History

Michael Roth, Editor
Getty Research Institute

NATIONALISM

Political Cultures in Europe and America, 1775–1865

Lloyd Kramer
University of North Carolina, Chapel Hill

Twayne Publishers
An Imprint of Simon & Schuster Macmillan
New York

Prentice Hall International
London • Mexico City • New Delhi • Singapore • Sydney • Toronto

Nationalism: Political Cultures in Europe and America, 1775–1865
Lloyd Kramer

Copyright © 1998 by Lloyd Kramer

Twayne Publishers
An Imprint of Simon & Schuster Macmillan
1633 Broadway
New York, NY 10019

Library of Congress Cataloging-in-Publication Data
Kramer, Lloyd S.
    Nationalism : political cultures in Europe and America, 1775–1865
/ Lloyd Kramer.
        p.   cm.   —(Studies in intellectual and cultural history)
    Includes bibliographical references and index.
    ISBN 0-8057-8610-4
    1. Nationalism—Europe.   2. Europe—History—1648–1789.
3. Europe—History—1789–1900.   4. Nationalism—United States.
5. United States—History—Revolution, 1775–1783.   6. United States—
History—1783–1865.   I. Title.   II. Series: Twayne's studies in
intellectual and cultural history.
D295.K73   1998
320.54′09182′109033—dc21   98-28089
                                                                        CIP

This paper meets the requirements of ANSI/NISO Z3948-1992
(Permanence of Paper).

10 9 8 7 6 5 4 3 2 1

Printed in the United States of America

Contents

Illustrations

Preface

Nationalism has decisively influenced world history for more than two centuries. Although it first developed its distinctive, modern characteristics in late-eighteenth-century America and Europe, it has spread rapidly across every part of the world, absorbing or displacing other ideologies such as romanticism, liberalism, conservatism, rationalism, socialism, and ancient religions. Nationalist movements and ideologies have produced or transformed most modern descriptions of human identity, and they have arguably contributed to more violent conflicts than any other political or ideological force in the contemporary world. Despite frequent predictions about nationalism's impending decline, people everywhere continue to define themselves in terms of their national origins and cultures.

Attempts to create a unified Europe face emotional opposition from nationalists in all the traditional European states, and the collapse of communist regimes in Eastern Europe has led to new, bloody nationalist conflicts in regions that were once "united" by official proclamations of socialist solidarity. Other nationalist conflicts dominate the news from various places in Africa, Asia, North America, and the Middle East. We now have numerous international agencies, vast networks of international commerce, constant migrations of people across national borders, and the mediating presence of the United Nations, but specific national identities and interests ultimately remain more important than internationalism for most people and all governments.

The exceptional power and prominence of nationalist movements have long attracted the scholarly attention of social scientists, political theorists, and historians as well as the commentaries of journalists and official policy makers, so the literature on nationalism can easily overwhelm anyone who wants to study its history. Much of this writing seeks to explain recent national conflicts and to describe the social, political, or economic demands of nationalist movements, but the discussion of contemporary conflicts often fails to provide enough historical perspective or enough analysis of the cultural traditions that shape nationalist identities. Faced with the immediate violence and bitterness of current events, many authors understandably write about present-day problems rather than the broader, complex cultural history of nationalist ideas.

While social scientists and journalists have been describing the politics or violence of modern nationalisms, however, other writers in the field of cultural studies have been developing an almost equally vast theoretical literature on the cultural construction of personal and group identities and the multiculturalism of contemporary societies. This innovative, new cultural approach to history and politics emphasizes the complex role of language, symbols, and narratives in the development and representation of the "self" and "others," thus reminding the social scientists that human actions always depend on human stories, ideas, and beliefs. Yet the new cultural studies of national identities have also tended to focus on contemporary issues and to discuss cultural identities in difficult, theoretical arguments that often drift away from specific historical evidence.

This book reflects and draws upon both the traditional scholarly concern with the power of nationalism and the recent theoretical debates about the cultural construction of identities, but it differs from much of this literature by examining the historical emergence of nationalism in Western societies during the era between the 1770s and 1860s. Historians have always recognized the importance of this era in the history of nationalism, but new cultural theories about the construction of memories, narratives, gender, and collective identities have opened new paths for the historical analysis of nationalist ideas. I therefore borrow from recent theories about cultural identities throughout this book, and yet (in contrast to many works in cultural studies) I give detailed attention to specific Western writers who helped create the modern meaning of nationalism in the decades during and after the American and French Revolutions.

This limited geographical and chronological framework obviously excludes most of the nationalist movements and conflicts in modern world history, but I think most nationalisms in other eras or places also express the cultural themes that I emphasize in the history of early European and American nationalisms: descriptions of national identity through accounts of national difference, claims for the political sovereignty of a "people," narratives about national history and culture, fusions with religious traditions, and presumptions about gender, families, or race.

Similar cultural and political patterns shape national identities and nationalisms in widely separated historical contexts, even when the manifestations of these nationalist patterns evolve in very different directions across time and cultures. This book thus examines recurring themes of nationalist thought with specific examples from early American and European nationalisms, and it mostly describes the similarities rather than the differences in New World and Old World nationalist ideologies. The emphasis on similarities in these nationalisms challenges traditional claims for American "exceptionalism"—claims that have often led Americans to assume that nationalism is something that happens "over there" in Germany or Eastern Europe or the Middle East. The early history of American nationalism, however, encompasses almost all the important cultural patterns of nationalist identities, so the American example can tell us a great deal about modern nationalism's emotional messages and political power.

It is much easier to recognize the nationalist cultural ideologies of other cultures than to recognize nationalism in one's own society. We all live in national contexts and absorb nationalist ideas every day of our lives, though we cannot identify the nationalism in these ideas without outside or alternative perspectives. Historical studies are therefore essential for anyone who sets out to understand nationalism in the contemporary world, because history provides the distancing perspective that enables us to describe the nationalist components in our own cultures and personal identities.

To summarize the guiding assumptions of this book in the most general terms, I think historical perspectives provide the indispensable starting point for the comprehension and criticism of modern nationalisms; and the careful study of specific historical events and texts shows how the most powerful cultural and emotional themes of present-day nationalist ideologies had already emerged in American and European nationalisms of the early nineteenth century.

Acknowledgments

I would like to thank my students for their insightful, challenging comments in courses on nationalism that I have taught at the University of North Carolina, Chapel Hill. Their wide-ranging cultural perspectives and experiences have given me a new understanding of how nationalist ideas influence the various levels of political, cultural, and personal life. I have also gained valuable new perspectives on the themes in this book from participants in the Sawyer Seminar on "Achieved Identities" at the National Humanities Center and from the members of seminars on nationalism that Professor Edward Tiryakian directs at Duke University.

I especially thank my colleagues Donald Reid and Jay Smith for their careful reading of the entire manuscript and for their helpful comments on my work. I also thank Timothy Riggs for his knowledgeable assistance on the illustrations, Michael Roth for his editorial encouragement, and Michelle Kovacs at Twayne Publishers for her energetic guidance.

Finally, I add my warmest appreciation to my wife, Gwynne Pomeroy, and my children, Kyle Kramer and Renee Kramer, for their support, encouragement, and good humor during the time I was working on this book. I have dedicated this book to Kyle and Renee, with the hope that historical understanding will help their generation reduce the intolerance of nationalist ideologies and the violence of nationalist conflicts.

1

The Cultural Meaning
of Nationalism

Nationalism has become the most widespread, influential political and cultural idea in the modern world because it gives people powerful stories to help them explain the meaning of their lives. The stories of nations appear everywhere in modern societies, including newspapers, schools, political debates, songs, sporting events, churches, advertisements for new cars, and recruitment campaigns for the military. Children grow up hearing stories about their nations, and virtually everyone defines identities with references to national cultures: "He is French, she is Russian, they are Japanese, we are Egyptians, I am American," and so on through every part of the world. National identities express deep human desires to participate in and identify with social communities, but these group identities have only acquired their distinctive nationalist meanings over the last two or three centuries.

Three stories from the early history of modern nations can introduce us to the cultural influence of nationalism. In September of 1776 a twenty-one-year-old man named Nathan Hale was executed by the British army in New York on charges of spying for America's new Continental Army. Hale thus became an early symbol of national sacrifice in the emerging American nationalism that was claiming its independence from Britain, and his famous last words became a moral lesson for every subsequent American generation: "I only regret that I have but one life to lose for my country."

In April of 1792 a soldier in the French army named Claude Joseph Rouget de Lisle sat down in Strasbourg to write a song about France's just-declared war with Prussia and Austria. Rouget de Lisle completed the song in a day, but its revolutionary call to arms became a permanent expression of French nationalism. "La Marseillaise" (as the song was soon called) resembles Hale's last words in stressing the virtues of sacrifice, and it describes the nation's cause as the highest duty for every citizen: "Let us go, children of the Fatherland / Our day of glory has arrived. / Against us stands tyranny / The bloody flag is raised; the bloody flag is raised."

In the winter of 1807 to 1808 the German philosopher Johann Gottlieb Fichte delivered a series of popular *Addresses to the German Nation* to large audiences in Berlin. Speaking shortly after the French army had taken control of his city, Fichte predicted that a new Germany would arise from this national humiliation. The French dominated Europe in 1807, but Fichte offered his audiences the philosophical assurance that decisive German actions would create a different future: "You will see in spirit the German name raised by means of this generation to be the most glorious among all peoples; you will see this nation the regenerator and re-creator of the world."[1]

The American spy, French songwriter, and German philosopher lived in different places, spoke different languages, and advocated different national causes, yet they shared a common historical role insofar as they contributed the language and exemplary actions for new nationalisms. Representing three social roles that all nationalisms require (martyr, lyricist, prophet), they all stressed the danger of enemies, the need for sacrifice, and the national ideal as the deepest source of identity. Their stories were connected with the revolutions and wars that first produced and expressed the modern ideas of nations and nationalism, and their lives point to the overlap of personal and public identities that has made nationalism so pervasive and powerful in modern world history. More generally, the actions and cultural memory of Hale, Rouget de Lisle, and Fichte exemplify the cultural construction of nationalism—the ubiquitous historical process that is the subject of this book.

Nationalism and Modernity

Most analysts of nationalism locate its emergence in late-eighteenth-century Europe. This argument for historical specificity challenges the typical nationalist's view of national identities as very old or even primordial realities, and it places nationalism at the center of political and cultural modernization. Where nationalisms usually claim to represent the deep spirit and traditions of common people, historians usually find the creation of nationalist ideas in the writings of elite intellectuals and political activists. People have always understood their lives in terms of their relations with local villages, families, religions, and geographical regions, but modern nationalisms emerged mostly in texts and in state institutions that promoted identifications with much larger territories and far more diverse populations.

Most historians therefore believe it is wrong to claim that nationalism expresses the traditional social values of long-existing social communities or that it represents essential racial and physical realities. In fact, nationalism grows out of and shapes modern social and political life, and it has no essential, metaphysical origin in ancient realities. As Hans Kohn noted in his classic study of the "idea" of nationalism, it "is first and foremost a state of mind, an act of consciousness," which is constructed like other ideas through constantly evolving historical conflicts, social relations, and political movements.[2] A more recent historian of nationalism, Liah Greenfeld, argues that nationalism is not simply the outcome of modernizing social and political institutions (e.g., capitalism and nation-states); it is instead the source of modernity. "Historically," Greenfeld explains, "the emergence of nationalism predated the development of every significant component of modernization." She therefore finds ideas about the nation shaping the history of countries such as England and France long before the late eighteenth century, but she insists that such ideas carry the seeds of modernity rather than the fruits of ancient or premodern national trees. Although other historians differ from Greenfeld by stressing the interplay of modern and premodern ideas or by inverting her account of the causal relation between modern social institutions and nationalist ideologies, the links between nationalism and modernity have become a widely accepted truism of historical explanation.[3]

The account of nationalism in this book draws on these perspectives to emphasize that national identities are historically constructed and that they developed their modern forms in late-eighteenth-century Europe and America. In contrast to many historians of Western nationalism, I link the themes of European nationalism to the emergence of nationalism in the United States, where the construction of national identity against an imperial European power might be compared to subsequent nationalisms in other regions of the world. Nationalism has always developed as a set of overlapping cultural and political ideas, all of which share the central assumption that the well-being and identity of individuals depend on their participation in a national culture. This assumption is the recurring cultural claim of nationalism, and it suggests the importance of nationalism for cultural historians. If the identity of individuals and groups is defined in terms of national cultures, then the historical construction of those cultures becomes crucial for understanding a whole range of historical issues—from politics and public conflicts to the interpretation of death or gender roles. The analysis here emphasizes the cultural dynamics of nationalism (the influence of language, history, religion, literature, and public symbols) instead of the social or military or economic history that might well be used to describe the emergence of nationalist institutions. Interest in the cultural construction of nationalism, however, does not simply negate other explanations for the popularity and power of modern nationalisms; in fact, the cultural approach to nationalism should also recognize the insights of alternative interpretations, including the ethnic and economic themes of recent social theorists.

The vehemence and violence of contemporary ethnic conflicts have prompted some analysts to question the modernity of nationalisms and to examine the premodern or ethnic origins of modern national identities. The English sociologist Anthony D. Smith, for example, complains that contemporary fascination with the cultural invention of nations causes historians to overlook the important limits on what intellectuals or politicians can actually claim for the cultural traditions of a nation. Nobody can simply construct a new national culture. The modern language of nationalism must refer to realities or experiences outside of writing, Smith argues, and these realities are actually found in the past experience of ethnic groups. Nationalism thus has deep roots, because "later generations of a particular community are formed in their collective life through the memories, myths and traditions of the community into which they are born and educated. . . . [T]hat past, as it is handed down from generation to generation in the form of subjective 'ethnohistory,' sets limits to current aspirations and perceptions." Smith assumes that this ethnohistory sets the parameters of national cultures and forces the would-be creators of a national identity to reconstruct the "traditions, customs and institutions of the ethnic community or communities which form the basis of the nation." Although he may lose sight of how rapidly languages and symbols can evolve, Smith's interest in continuities and the premodern roots of national identities offers an important critical alternative to the current emphasis on the modern cultural construction of nationalisms.[4]

Another influential alternative to the recent cultural history of nationalism appears in the work of Ernest Gellner, who (unlike Smith) argues for the radical novelty of modern nationalism and who (unlike most cultural historians) argues for the economic origins of nationalism. Gellner sees nationalism as the practical solution to the needs of industrializing modern societies, whose complex economies require specialized divisions of labor, educated workers who communicate across long distances, and mobile populations that read the same language and follow the same laws. Nationalism provides the rationale and institutions for this educated, mobile workforce as it creates the standardized languages, schools, and technical training that separate industrialized nations from traditional agrarian cultures. "The roots of nationalism in the distinctive structural requirements of industrial society are very deep indeed," Gellner argues. Nationalism is therefore a product of modernizing economies, and it appears when the social structures of a culture begin to evolve away from the relatively stable, hierarchical relations of peasant communities. "It is not the case . . . that nationalism imposes homogeneity; it is rather that a homogeneity imposed by objective, inescapable imperative eventually appears on the surface in the form of nationalism."[5]

Gellner's economic structuralism carries an important reminder that politics and culture are always connected with economic life, yet his economic explanations fail to account for the complexity of national cultures or the emotional passions that such cultures regularly generate. The cultural meanings of nationalism go beyond economic modernization into nuances of language, history, and religion that have little or no value for standardized labor forces, though they create identities for which people are willing to kill and die. Indeed, Smith's search for continuities with premodern ethnic cultures may tell us more about the powerful, emotional attraction of nationalism than we can learn from Gellner's account of economic modernization. But if economic imperatives cannot adequately account for the meanings of national cultures, how do nationalisms and modern cultures come together in the overlapping personal and public spheres of individual lives?

Cultures and Identities

People always have multiple identities. They describe themselves (and are described by others) with reference to their positions in families, work, professional status, wealth, gender, race, education, religious affiliations, and political allegiances—not to mention other identities such as loyalties to athletic teams or club memberships or hometowns. All of these identities depend on relations and interactions with other people, and many have been part of human experience since the beginning of civilization. Nationalism does not usually deny or displace other forms of personal identity, but it typically defines national identity as the essential identity that gives coherence to all other aspects of a person's life. The ascribed traits of nationality are used to define virtually every level of public and private life, so that we hear about "Italian" families, "German" workers, "American" Protestants, "Chinese" food, or maybe a "French" kiss.

Nations are thus organizing cultural categories that structure, regulate, and contribute meanings to most of the actions and relationships through which we understand our lives. Loyalty to nations "flourishes," as the historian David Potter has explained, "not by challenging and overpowering all other loyalties, but by subsuming them all and keeping them in a reciprocally supportive relationship to one another."[6] This implicit nationalism in the relationships of everyday life becomes more explicit and coercive during wars, when national governments demand the lives of young people and the labor, wealth, or disciplined loyalty of entire societies. Nationalism provides the justification for such modern mobilizations, but it can also be found, notes Peter Alter, "whenever individuals feel they belong primarily to the nation, and whenever affective attachment and loyalty to that nation override all other attachments and loyalties."[7] Indeed, nationalists believe that most human activities and attachments acquire significance through their connections with a nation: "family values" and "religious morality," for example, may be celebrated as essential to the survival of a strong national culture, whereas a declining commitment to marriage or religion may be interpreted as the cause of national weakness and decline.

Modern nationalism provides more than reinforcement of traditional families or religions, however, because it can also compensate for the breakdown of traditional social, cultural, and religious attachments. Identifying with the power of a nation may become a consolation or replacement for losses and disappointments that accompany the growth of modern cities, economic institutions, and social mobility. The sociologist Liah Greenfeld, for example, argues that a social and cultural "identity crisis" has preceded the embrace of nationalism in every modern society. Set free from the hierarchies and social categories of traditional cultures, individuals and groups in modernizing societies have regularly experienced what Greenfeld calls a sense of social "anomie" and disorientation. Fervent nationalists often emerge in such contexts, transforming strong resentments about the lack of recognition for their work, social status, or social group into passionate claims for national achievement and superiority. Identity is a crucial issue here as in every cultural ideal, but the nationalist identity for Greenfeld has frequently been an identity for the unrecognized, the isolated, or the unhappy intellectual—all of whom have turned to nationalism as the empowering solution for their own frustrations. "Wherever it [*ressentiment*] existed," Greenfeld writes, "it fostered particularistic pride and xenophobia, providing emotional nourishment for the nascent national sentiment and sustaining it whenever it faltered."[8]

National identities emerged as cultural constructions that lacked the long history of traditional social hierarchies and religions, yet they enabled otherwise alienated persons to identify with a power beyond themselves and their own situation. "Nationality makes people feel good," Greenfeld explains, especially when it promotes a "collectivistic nationalism" that allows individuals "to partake in the dignity of a far greater, stronger, and more perfect being, the brilliance of whose virtues has the power to blind one to one's own failings."[9] Nationalist narratives thus stress the coherence and unity of the nation (much like religious narratives describe the unity of God), thereby offering access to coherence and unity for individuals whose lives might be threatened by the fragmentation and incoherence of modern social life. The much-desired coherence of national identities produces repression as well as consolation, however, because the belief in unified national cultures has often justified attacks on people who resist or stand outside the utopian aspiration for full coherence. Strong national identities can mean that every perceived threat to the nation becomes also a threat to individual identities—and a rationale for repression.

The history of nationalist violence and attempted "purifications" has provoked some critics to condemn all forms of nationalism, but the pervasive influence of national cultures in the modern world calls for a more complex response and question: How can people acknowledge and affirm national identities without lapsing into the totalizing claims and repressions of the fervent nationalist? Seeking answers to this question, the contemporary study of national identities has turned away from the nationalists' aspiration for full coherence to emphasize the multiple identities that challenge all desires for a completely unified nation (or individual). This multicultural view of nations produces a new history of nationalism and the construction of national identities. Where nationalists stress the deep reality and coherence of national identity, the multicultural analysis of nationalism stresses difference and multiplicity. The personal and the collective are still connected, but the connections are seen as ambiguous, unstable, and always evolving. Reduced to its most basic theme, the multicultural argument denies the existence of essential, unified national identities.

This emphasis on difference rather than essence in the construction of nationalist identities opens a new historical approach to the never-ending process of national identity formation. As the cultural theorist Stuart Hall explains in a concise account of national cultures, this identity "is not something which already exists, transcending place, time, history, and culture. Cultural identities come from somewhere, have histories." The history of nationalism in this view—and it is also the theme of this book—becomes a history of constant cultural reconstruction because each generation must extend and redefine the meaning of the nation. A national cultural identity, to continue with Hall's themes, "is always constructed through memory, fantasy, narrative and myth. Cultural identities are . . . the unstable points of identification or suture, which are made within the discourses of history and culture. Not an essence but a *positioning.*" Equally important, this continual positioning of national cultures carries the legacy of multiple cultures, the multicultural reality that exceeds and defies traditional nationalist narratives of pure national origins and simple beginnings. Hall's description of Afro-Caribbean people who descend from the African diaspora could also apply to virtually every modern national culture. "The diaspora experience . . . is defined, not by essence or purity, but by the recognition of a necessary heterogeneity and diversity; by a conception of 'identity' which lives with and through, not despite difference; by *hybridity.*"[10]

The search for hybrid, diverse levels of culture that converge and diverge in national identities has generated new studies of the cultural and social *interactions* that create identities for individuals and groups alike. All such interactions evolve through the languages, symbols, and narratives that define and spread ideas about the meaning of a nation. The last words of Nathan Hale, the song of Rouget de Lisle, and the lectures of J. G. Fichte, for example, would have no historical or cultural significance without the narratives and symbols that carried each text into the cultural memory of a nation. Growing interest in these processes of cultural construction and diffusion has therefore brought the study of nationalism into a new cultural history of the languages and symbols that construct the meaning of all social realities.

Nationalism and Cultural History

Cultural historians have challenged an earlier conception of written documents (which assumed that writing reflects or describes reality) by arguing that language and writing actively construct social reality. This "new" cultural history does not deny the existence of a material world, yet it stresses that material objects can have no meaning for people without the words and cultural values that we use to organize, compare, describe, remember, and understand every object or person we encounter. Language creates connections between sensory experiences, establishes hierarchies of significance, and brings philosophical assumptions into the most mundane actions of daily life.[11] If human beings lost language, they would also lose their history, memory, and culture; and this linguistic heart of cultural life leads some theorists to claim that the history of the world as we know it is really a history of language.

Although few historians are inclined to call the world a text, the contemporary emphasis on the dynamic, shaping force of language has pushed them to give close attention to the words and symbols that define and construct social relations, political movements, religions, wars, and the exercise of power. This historical search for linguistic meaning influences the study of social transitions such as the growth of cities and the creation of industrial technology, but it has become even more prominent in the study of ideas such as nationalism. Nations do not exist in nature. They are created by human cultures, and they provide a conspicuous example of how human realities develop through languages, symbols, and imaginative narratives.

The cultural construction of nations dominates daily life in forms that we assimilate with little or no conscious reflection: in maps, flags, money, stamps, public buildings and monuments, museums, passports, songs, history books, school examinations, religious services, uniforms, youth scout groups, political constitutions, elections, military service, newspaper stories, weather reports, films, television shows, advertisements, and military cemeteries. This list by no means includes all the spheres of culture that create and re-create modern nations, but it is long enough to suggest why cultural history has become so influential in the study of nationalism.

Current debates about nationalism's cultural history draw theories and examples from anthropology, sociology, and literary studies as well as from social and political history, thus generating a vast literature that can overwhelm even the most indefatigable reader. Among the many recent publications in this genre, however, I will mention three that have been especially influential in shaping contemporary research and also the conceptual framework of this book.

The first is the important work by Benedict Anderson, *Imagined Communities,* which has become the provocative starting point for commentaries on all kinds of cultural and national identities. Anderson describes nations as distinctive modern constructions that emerge when people imagine themselves to be closely affiliated, though they never meet and though they may differ widely in education, work, income, and personal beliefs. The nation nevertheless brings these diverse populations to a shared identity, writes Anderson, in "an imagined political community" that is "imagined as both inherently limited and sovereign."

This national community is much larger than traditional families, villages, and geographical regions, but it becomes imaginable for people who read the stories of nations in the schools, newspapers, and novels of modern, centralizing states and colonies. Anderson's influential account of the modern nation is best summarized in his own well-known definitions:

> [The nation] is *imagined* because the members of even the smallest nation will never know most of their fellow-members, meet them, or even hear of them, yet in the minds of each lives the image of their communion. . . . In fact, all communities larger than primordial villages of face-to-face contact (and perhaps even these) are imagined. Communities are to be distinguished, not by their falsity/genuineness, but by the style in which they are imagined. . . .
>
> The nation is imagined as *limited* because even the largest of them . . . has finite, if elastic boundaries, beyond which lie other nations. . . .
>
> It is imagined as *sovereign* because the concept was born in an age in which Enlightenment and Revolution were de-

stroying the legitimacy of the divinely-ordained, hierarchical dynastic realm. . . .

Finally, it is imagined as a *community*, because, regardless of the actual inequality and exploitation that may prevail in each, the nation is always conceived as a deep, horizontal comradeship.[12]

Anderson's account of the cultural imagination provides a paradigm for understanding how nations unite widely dispersed populations and how these imagined (but real) identifications produce emotional passions and consolations for the pains of life and death. His conception of the imagined community—constructed in language, emerging first in eighteenth-century revolutions, and generating both personal and collective identities—reappears often in this book.

A related conceptual model for understanding nationalisms is developed in the essays that Eric Hobsbawm and Terence Ranger collected for publication in *The Invention of Tradition*.[13] Although Hobsbawm and Ranger resemble Anderson in assuming that nations are constructed through symbolic, imaginative processes, the essays in their book often suggest a more self-conscious development of "invented traditions" that are supposed to express continuities with a national past. Nationalists regularly claim to speak the essential truth of the nation, but Hobsbawm stresses "the peculiarity of 'invented' traditions," whose much affirmed continuity with the historic past is "largely fictitious." Strangely enough, entirely modern national identities and nation-states seek legitimacy with references to a premodern or natural order. Such ritual invocations of tradition mask the radical novelty of what was in fact invented by the public actions of specific people in a specific era, most notably the nineteenth century.[14] Hobsbawm may assume too much coherence in these invented traditions, and he overlooks the cultural continuities that give new traditions their meaning. His emphasis on the dynamic creation of modern national rituals has nevertheless stimulated innovative new research on the symbols, monuments, and histories that sustain the nationalist account of "old" national traditions.

Imagined communities and invented traditions now provide the thematic structure for many studies of nationalism, but the theories of Anderson and Hobsbawm have been extended and redefined in the literary essays of Homi Bhabha's edited collection, *Nation and Narration*. Whereas Anderson and Hobsbawm express the traditional historian's desire to describe the coherence of past cultures, Bhabha and his colleagues express the recent literary desire to uncover the fragments, tensions, and incoherences of past or contemporary texts. Bhabha draws on poststructuralist themes to argue that nations are like other imaginary texts: They are narrated by authors who strive for a coherence and order that can never be fully achieved. Narratives about an imagined community cannot create the national purity and clarity that their authors desire because entirely coherent communities (and texts) do not exist. The inescapable differences within a nation's imaginary boundaries stymie the quest for national homogeneity, Bhabha explains, though the differences are also needed to sustain the meaning of the nation.

Narrating a national identity is thus at the center of all nationalisms, yet this narrative (like the narratives in other texts) cannot finally master what it seeks to describe. "Counter-narratives of the nation that continually evoke and erase its totalizing boundaries . . . disturb those ideological manoeuvres through which 'imagined communities' are given essentialist identities." Although Bhabha's prose is difficult to read, his themes are important. Nationalism is a form of "writing" that seeks to transform the "cultural difference and the heterogeneous histories of contending peoples" into a unified cultural reality.[15] The inevitable obstacles to the final success of this project give nationalism an endless campaign and a constant need to rewrite the nation in every generation; nationalists, in short, cannot reach the total national coherence and unity they imagine and seek.

Bhabha therefore expands the cultural history of nationalism beyond Anderson and Hobsbawm with two important themes: (1) narratives about the nation fail to achieve a much desired literary and political coherence, in part because (2) the meaning of all such narratives depends on the presence of both internal and external differences that can never disappear. Definitions of the nation, like all other ideas, develop through polarities that nationalists see as clear, distinct, and oppositional but whose meanings are always already entangled with the differences they theoretically oppose. The meaning of "German," for example, emerges through interactions with the "French," and the category "white" derives meaning from its relation to "black."

Nationalism and Difference

The new cultural history of national identities thus develops the antiessentialist assumption that identities are always relational. Definitions of nations depend on definitions of difference and on relations with other cultures, so that the imaginary essence of a nation evolves as the definitions of difference and cultural boundaries evolve. "National identity," Peter Sahlins writes in a concise summary, "is a socially constructed and continuous process of defining 'friend' and 'enemy.' "[16] This evolving description of difference suggests why a change in friends or enemies also changes the meaning of a nation's identity. The end of the Cold War, for example, affected America's national identity because the demise of the Soviet Union removed a clearly defined enemy that had helped to sustain the unity of American nationalism.

The influence of *difference* in the construction of national identities leads to the guiding theme of this book: Nationalisms are cultural and political ideologies that claim distinctive, superior identities for

Napoleon at Arcis-Sur-Aube. Woodcut by François Georgin, 1836. Ackland Art Museum, The University of North Carolina, Chapel Hill, Burton Emmett Collection.

Images of national difference often refer to military conflicts because warfare marks the clearest boundaries between nations. Georgin's illustration of a famous battle scene from the last phase of the Napoleonic Wars (1814) portrays Napoleon leading French troops against an invading Prussian army, but the deeper nationalist message suggests a stark division between France and a threatening foreign enemy.

groups of people whose history, institutions, and ideals are said to *differ* in crucial respects from other cultures and human societies. Nationalisms typically carry strong political aspirations for existing nation-states or for social groups that seek identity and independence through the establishment of new nation-states. In every case, however, the existence of a nation depends on cultural and political boundaries that separate insiders from outsiders.

Each chapter of this book refers to the use of *difference* in distinctive (though connected) spheres of nationalist thought and practice. This recurring theme appears, among other places, in the rituals of national political cultures; the praise for national languages, histories, and literatures; the affirmation of national religions; and the nationalist definitions of gender, race, or ethnicity. All nationalisms require these identity-shaping cultural actions, but they develop remarkably different institutions and accounts of their national achievements. Following and expressing the history of these widely defined differences, histories of nationalism often resemble the national identities they describe by drawing sharp contrasts between various forms of nationalist culture and political action. Such contrasts are needed for historical understanding, yet they should not obscure the nearly universal belief in national differences that shapes the emergence and survival of every modern nationalism.

Varieties of Nationalism

Historians have been categorizing nationalisms and national identities since the early twentieth century, striving to find historical patterns in political and cultural movements that regularly claim to be unique. Although the contributors to this debate often disagree about appropriate analytical categories, nationalisms are given their historical meaning through oppositions such as Western/Eastern, political/cultural, old/new, liberal/conservative, and civic/ethnic. These oppositional categories help historians compare and identify various phases of nationalism, but they also tend to convey a strong ethical distinction between good and bad. Nationalisms that express the good side of these oppositions (Western, political, old, liberal, and civic) are usually identified in countries such as England, France, and the United States. Nationalisms that express the bad side of the ideology (Eastern, cultural, new, conservative, and ethnic) are generally linked to countries such as Germany, Slavic Eastern Europe, or anticolonial states in Asia and Africa. Historians must make analytical distinctions and identify differences between various national cultures, but they must also use such categories critically to avoid the simple replication of nationalist assumptions in their own cultures.

Analytical categories in contemporary histories of nationalism, for example, still express historical responses to the horrors of Nazism or the brutalities of colonial wars or the violence of ethnic cleansing. Attempts to understand such events have generated repeated commentary on the differences between Western nationalisms and Eastern nationalisms, usually stressing the difference between beliefs in universal human rights and beliefs in a specific national culture. The first form of nationalism, which is often called liberal nationalism (Liah Greenfeld's term is *individualistic-libertarian*), typically includes individual rights in its definition of the nation's fundamental ideals. The second form of nationalism, often called integral nationalism (Greenfeld's term is *collectivistic-authoritarian*), typically subsumes the individual into a national community and identifies the nation in terms of race or culture rather than politics and individual rights.[17] The civic, political nation is theoretically open to newcomers because individuals can choose to join the civic nation, whereas the ethnic, linguistic nation is theoretically closed to outsiders because individuals are *born into* ethnic and linguistic communities.

This schematic model of contrasting nationalisms has long enabled historians to separate France from Germany or Western Europe from Eastern Europe, but it also offers categories to explain different forms of nationalism within a single national culture. One common argument notes, for example, that nationalism was mainly an ideology of liberals and the political left until the mid–nineteenth century, when the political right began to embrace nationalist ideas in the name of conservatism and tradition. Nationalism in France and Germany could thus be civic or political in one context, and ethnic or linguistic in another. Similarly, nationalism could be the ideology of left-wing anticolonialist movements or the ideological justification for conservative regimes in postcolonial states. In short, nationalism moves widely across the political spectrum, sometimes promoting universal ideas such as human rights and sometimes promoting the extreme particularism of ideas such as racial superiority.

Emphasizing the differences in nationalisms thus brings order to the contradictory themes within and among nationalist movements, but the chronology of nationalism almost always locates its early emergence in the political ideas of the American and French Revolutions. These revolutions claimed national sovereignty for the "people" rather than for kings or social elites, and a rhetorical claim to represent the "people" would become the political theme of every subsequent nationalism. Yet this early political claim, as most analysts describe it, evolved into a much stronger cultural claim as it was redefined in Germany and other societies to the east. Nationalisms in Eastern Europe and in other societies of Asia and Africa thus appear in most Western narratives as derivative variations of the claims for national sovereignty that emerged first in the West.[18] It is important to recognize the historical differences among nationalisms and also to give close attention to diverse forms of political and cultural nationalisms. There are, for example, crucial differences between the rationale and objectives of the political violence in the French Revolution and the racist violence in Nazi Germany, though both forms of violence have some relation to nationalist ideologies. Despite the importance of historical differences, however, the cultural history of nationalism in this book emphasizes the ideas that nationalisms share rather than the political, economic, and military actions that make them different.

My cultural approach to nationalism gives particular attention to three national cultures: the "old" nation in France, a society whose national identity is usually described as an example of political nationalism; the "old" or "new" nation in Germany, a society whose national identity is usually described as a cultural or ethnic nationalism; and the "new" nation in the United States, a society whose national identity is usually described as a political nationalism (which brought together an otherwise diverse immigrant population). Setting aside some of the familiar distinctions between "old" and "new" nations, I stress similarities in the cultural component of political nationalisms and the political component of cultural nationalisms. More specifically, I look at how each of these national cultures defined identities against difference and developed their nationalist ideas through the active power of new national narratives. Where much of the literature on nationalism points to the diversity of nationalist movements, this book emphasizes similarities.

The Emergence of Nationalism in an Age of Revolutions

The similarity in different nationalisms becomes especially notable in the emergence of specific Western European and American nationalisms during the era of early democratic revolutions (1775–1850). The "age of democratic revolutions" was also the first age of nationalist revolutions, a link that suggests how much nationalism (even in its authoritarian forms) owes to the antiaristocratic idea of democratic national sovereignty.[19] Early nationalisms have of course been transformed by modern forms of communication, worldwide movements against colonialism, new kinds of violence and warfare, and other social movements such as socialism and communism. The changing contexts of nationalism, however, have not decisively altered the deep structures of cultural interaction that create modern nationalisms and national identities.

This book therefore examines European and American cultural and political movements that drew on Western religious traditions, the eighteenth-century Enlightenment, contemporary revolutions, and Romantic philosophy to construct new nationalist ideologies. Needless to say, these nationalisms are not the only influential national movements in the modern world, but the identity-shaping cultural processes in their writings, ideas, and political actions can be found in the diverse nationalisms of every subsequent generation and in every part of the world. The cultural meaning of nationalism—defined through dynamic conceptions of difference and narrated in famous texts such as the last words of Nathan Hale or "The Marsaillaise" or the *Addresses to the German Nation*—developed rapidly during the last decades of the eighteenth century. The cultural history of nationalism thus begins with (and still assumes) the sovereign power of the "people," whose commanding presence was first proclaimed in the languages of the American and French Revolutions.

2

Nationalism, Politics, and Revolutions

Modern nationalisms have differed widely in their descriptions of national ideals and traditions, but virtually every nationalism has developed political objectives and political institutions. Nationalisms always describe specific groups of people and almost always claim that such groups must be represented by their own political states, political institutions, and political organizations. The modern nationalisms that developed in the late eighteenth century thus promoted new views of the proper relation between governments and the people whom they control, stressing that national communities must be represented and protected by nation-states. This new concept of nations described a political identity that differed from older political entities such as empires (which often ruled diverse cultures and linguistic groups), city-states (which typically represented only small territories within larger cultures and linguistic groups), or traditional monarchies (which claimed legitimacy on grounds of family lineage or divine right rather than the will of a nation). The political novelty of nationalism thus developed through the assumption that state power should represent a coherent group of "people" who live inside a well-defined territory.

Although such ideas had occasionally appeared in Europe since the sixteenth century (for example, in some of Machiavelli's aspirations for Italy in the 1520s or in the English Protestant response to the Spanish Armada in the 1580s), distinctive *democratic* claims about the sovereignty of nations emerged most clearly in the American and French Revolutions. The revolutionary conflicts in France were especially important in shaping new accounts of the "nation" as a political community that expressed both the sovereignty and will of a large, but specific, national population. Strong claims for distinctive cultural identities in later nationalisms may have obscured the two essential political themes of eighteenth-century revolutionary nationalisms: The sovereignty of a nation lies in its people rather than in a king or social elites, and these sovereign nations (as well as the individuals who live in them) have certain fundamental rights to liberty and equality. Elite social groups had sometimes argued that they represented the nation against monarchs in England and France, but the American and French Revolutions established new forms of national identity by claiming to represent the sovereign will of an entire nation.[1]

Ideas about national sovereignty and human rights emerged in new political theories, economic relations, and cultural institutions, all of which became part of the eighteenth-century Enlightenment. The critical thinkers who contributed to this famous, secularizing cultural movement—from John Locke to Montesquieu, Voltaire, and Jean-Jacques Rousseau—all challenged the traditional assumption that kings ruled by divine right. The "sacred monarch," notes Hans Kohn in his intellectual history of this early modern transition, "lost his symbolic value as the center and justification of society." This loss of legitimating, divine-right sovereignty occurred gradually over time, but the critique of royal sovereignty also carried a new positive claim for the political legitimacy that came entirely from the "people." This claim presumed a contract between governments and the governed, though the "people" could generate even more social and political meanings than a king could. "The sovereignty of the prince who had been one," Kohn explains, "was to be replaced by the sovereignty of the people, who had to become one in a higher sense of the word."[2]

This new sovereign entity would be entitled to freedoms that had once been reserved for sovereign kings. The people of each nation, for example, had to be independent of external control to act on their collective national will, and this national independence could not be secure until it was embodied in a national state. Nobody summarized this new guiding theory of political life more forcefully than

Jean-Jacques Rousseau (1712–1778), who argued that collective and personal identities came together in the "general will" of the nation. *"Each of us places his person and all his power in common under the supreme direction of the general will,"* Rousseau wrote in *The Social Contract* (1762); *"and as one we receive each member as an indivisible part of the whole."* This general will was the basis of national sovereignty, which for Rousseau was "inalienable" and "indivisible." The nation's sovereign existence thus acquired divine qualities that earlier generations had found in God and in kings. As Rousseau explained it, "since sovereignty is merely the exercise of the general will, it can never be alienated, and . . . the sovereign, which is only a collective being, cannot be represented by anything but itself."[3] The first political meaning of nationalism (though Rousseau did not call this idea "nationalism") therefore emphasized the collective reality and political will of a sovereign community that was to be represented by a state. As for the individuals within this community, they could find the meaning and freedom of their lives through connections to the sovereign state in much the same way that Christianity had found the purpose and meaning of individuals in their connections to God.

Although the political claims of Rousseau and other theorists may suggest that individuals would have no more freedom under sovereign nations than under sovereign kings, the new definitions of national sovereignty were often linked to new definitions of human rights. Enlightenment ideas about human reason required that individuals, like sovereign peoples, should have the rights to pursue the truth freely, no matter where the inquiry might lead in religion, society, or politics. These rights were eventually defined in theoretical detail during the late-eighteenth-century revolutions, but the early modern definition of natural rights had been developing throughout the previous century. The breakdown of religious unity after the Protestant Reformation and the breakdown of divine-right monarchy after the emergence of Enlightenment-era political theory provided an opening for new definitions of individual knowledge and personal autonomy. Challenges to the traditional religious and monarchical foundations of the European political order also overlapped with economic and social changes that were weakening another traditional base of European society—the hierarchical social order that had long defined different rights and duties for nobles and commoners. A new social world evolved with the economic assumptions and policies of early capitalism. Put simply, the social theories in this emerging economic system became linked with new political theories in calling for the reward of individual merit and enterprise (the ideology that historians have often labeled "individualism") and in generating new descriptions of the ideal state as a protector of individual rights as well as collective interests. By the late eighteenth century, therefore, one finds a complex interaction between what Louis Dumont calls the "holism" of traditional social life and the "individualism" of modernizing social relations.[4] These interactions produced constant conflicts and social fusions, including new holistic nationalisms that defined their purposes and identities in the language of individual rights.

The late-eighteenth-century revolutions thus tended to combine theories of national rights and sovereign independence with declara-

The Triumph of Liberty. Oil on canvas by Jacques Réattu, 1793–94. Musée Réattu, Arles. Photograph by Michel Lacanaud.
Supporters of the French Revolution celebrated this event as the victory of liberty—represented in this typical revolutionary painting as a woman carrying the tricolor flag and protected by heroic, classical soldiers. The sovereign power of nations, however, often overwhelmed the theoretical freedom of individuals and created conflicts that Réattu's work could not resolve.

tions about individual rights and liberties—though the possible contradictions between the rights of nations and the rights of individuals soon became apparent in recurring conflicts over issues such as slavery, warfare, and the repression of dissent. Rousseau expressed the contradictions that could readily appear in the overlapping claims for collective sovereignty and individual freedom (individuals who failed to accept the general will could "be forced to be free"), but he also submerged such problems in his confident affirmations of the sovereign nation's social equality. "The social compact," Rousseau explained, "establishes among the citizens an equality of such a kind that they all commit themselves under the same conditions and should all enjoy the same rights. Thus by the very nature of the compact, every act of sovereignty (that is, every authentic act of the general will) obligates or favors all citizens equally, so that the sovereign knows only the nation as a body and does not draw distinctions between any of those members that make it up."[5]

Nationalism and individualism therefore evolved as related but also conflicting ideologies of human rights in the revolutionary political cultures of the era. To return to the classic political explanations of Hans Kohn,

> In the eighteenth century the free personality emerged in all fields of human activity. . . . But this new order posited the grave problem of how to conciliate the liberty of the individual with the exigencies of social integration, how to subject man to a law which could no longer claim the authority of an absolute lawgiver outside and above men. In this situation nationalism was to become the tie binding the autonomous individual into the partnership of a community.[6]

Rousseau's writings provided in this context a new account of sovereignty (the general will) and of individual liberty (freedom realized in collective action) that would help fuse new conceptions of the nation with older religious or political allegiances in a new realm of revolutionary politics. The idea of the nation offered political integration for a liberal society whose religious unity had disappeared, whose monarchs had lost legitimacy, and whose individuals no longer deferred to a clearly delineated social hierarchy. Nationalism thus offered (from the beginning and in subsequent eras) a new structure for political order and social identity during the political and social transition to modernity.[7]

The key political themes of national sovereignty and human rights suggest the novelty of nationalism and also its role in modernizing social processes. It was by no means a throwback to an earlier era. On the contrary, nationalist revolutions and movements began by defining their differences from the old, from what had come before. Nationalist movements generally sought to separate themselves from "old regime" social and political institutions that were denounced for impeding the freedom of the nation and the individuals who composed it. Such revolutions looked optimistically to a future that would differ from the old regime policies of Britain's monarchy, France's royal bureaucracy, or Germany's scattered princely states. The early political history of nationalism was thus mostly liberal and revolutionary rather than conservative or reactionary, in large part because the demands for popular national sovereignty and human rights challenged the traditional political order. But to understand how these claims could move from political theory into new governments and national movements in America and Europe, we must look at specific examples of late-eighteenth-century nationalist ideas and practice, all of which depended on the new language and symbols of national identity.

Nationalism in the American Revolution

The characteristic political patterns of most modern nationalisms—claims for national sovereignty, claims for human rights, critiques of old regime governments—first appeared prominently in the American Revolution. Although historians have often assumed that nationalism emerged first in late-eighteenth-century Europe, many of the early statements of modern political nationalism can actually be found in the ideological justifications for America's revolutionary war against Britain. As Benedict Anderson notes in his persuasive account of America's "creole" nationalisms, "It is an astonishing sign of the depth of Eurocentrism that so many European scholars persist, in the face of all the evidence, in regarding nationalism as a European invention."[8] Nationalism emerged gradually in the culture, religion, and economy of the Euro-American society that became the United States of America (see chapter 6), but the major identity-shaping texts of the revolutionary era show that Americans described their war with Britain as a *political* struggle for national sovereignty and independence.

The American Declaration of Independence, for example, listed specific grievances to justify an armed insurrection, yet the most striking passages of that famous document insisted more generally on the sovereignty and rights of the American people. "We hold these truths to be self-evident," wrote Thomas Jefferson, "that all men are created equal, that they are endowed by their Creator with certain unalienable Rights, that among these are Life, Liberty and the Pursuit of Happiness." Jefferson thus began with assertions about individual freedom that would reappear in other nationalist movements, but the claim for individual rights led immediately to a connected claim for the importance of national governments. "That to secure these rights, Governments are instituted among Men, deriving their just powers from the consent of the governed, That whenever any Form of Government becomes destructive of these ends, it is the Right of the People to alter or to abolish it, and to institute new Government, laying its foundation on such principles and organizing its powers in such form, as to them shall seem most to effect their Safety and Happiness." This theoretical argument for the sovereign "People" of America provided the rationale for establishing a new nation and new political institutions such as the Continental Congress. "We, therefore, the Representatives of the United States of America, in General Congress . . . do, in the Name, and by Authority of the good People of these Colonies, solemnly publish and declare, That these United Colonies are, and of Right ought to be Free and Independent States."[9] America's Declaration of Independence thus offered a powerful rhetorical summary of how national governments should express the sovereign rights of a "good People" and provided an organizing theme for most other early American national narratives, including the popular works of Thomas Paine (1737–1809), David Ramsay (1749–1815), and Philip Freneau (1752–1832).

Paine's arguments for national independence appeared in *Common Sense* (1776), an influential political pamphlet that offered the most vehement rationale for a definitive American separation from Britain. Complaining that "the good people" of America were "greviously oppressed" by the British government, Paine helped transform the local political conflicts of an emerging nation into a cause with universal significance. He thus promoted a nationalist theme (the exceptional nation offers redemption for others) that would become common in European nationalist movements throughout the next century. "The cause of America is in a great measure the cause of all mankind," Paine noted in his call for national independence. "The laying a Country desolate with Fire and Sword, declaring War against the natural rights of all Mankind, and extirpating the Defenders thereof from the Face of the Earth, is the Concern of every Man to whom Nature hath given the Power of feeling." America's Revolution represented for Paine (and his many sympathetic readers) a decisive struggle between the new and the old, freedom and oppression, national sovereignty and monarchical power. "O ye that love mankind," wrote Paine, "Ye that dare oppose, not only the tyranny, but the tyrant, stand forth! Every spot of the old world is overrun with oppression." Standing against this decadent Old World history, the New World offered a refuge for freedom and all those who wanted more freedom in their lives. "O receive the fugitive, and prepare in time an asylum for mankind."[10] Paine thus imagined an ambitious political mission for this small, isolated new nation, but the ambition and optimism in his narrative helped create an imagined community that would define itself through its opposition to the corruption and oppression of long-established European states.

Paine's themes were repeated throughout the Revolution as American writers explained the meaning of the battles and the political objectives of the war. A new nationalist narrative contrasted America's defense of freedom and popular sovereignty with the repressive policies of Old World monarchs and gave the Continental Army a world-historical purpose. David Ramsay's "Oration on American Independence" (July 4, 1778), for example, helped to launch rituals of celebration for the nation's unique achievements and identity. Calling America's war "the Cause of Human Nature," Ramsay assured an audience in South Carolina that "Our independence will redeem one quarter of the globe from tyranny and oppression, and consecrate it the chosen seat of truth, justice, freedom, and religion."[11] The deaths in battle and the daily miseries of soldiers thus took on transcendent meaning and purpose in a developing story of American national identity, which explained why Americans must wage war for their independence and how they differed from the British enemy they were fighting.

The revolutionary poems of Philip Freneau transformed the prose of Paine and the oratory of Independence Day speakers into a poetic commentary on the moral dichotomies of the Revolution. Celebrating the naval victories of the American commander John Paul Jones (1781), for example, Freneau used the "brave Jones," to explain the political meaning of the war: "The rights of men demand thy care: / For *these* you dare the greedy waves." No monarch could withstand such a principled national opponent, Freneau argued, so the British "to our Thirteen Stars shall bend" and the "radiant" American flag would soon "ascend."[12] The final military victory at Yorktown confirmed the truth of such nationalist predictions, and the American Revolution moved quickly from the identity-shaping narratives of warfare to the identity-shaping narratives of historical memory.

American writers therefore described the superiority of their new nation in political texts that linked the American right of national sovereignty to wider definitions of universal human rights. This kind of nationalism, as its advocates predicted, provided a revolutionary example for people outside America who wanted to change their governments, and most American nationalists embraced the French Revolution in 1789 as a European expression of the principles that had shaped their own war for national independence. Freneau welcomed the revolutionary French ambassador to Philadelphia in 1793 with strong praise for the ideas of popular sovereignty and republicanism that now united France and America. "Thanks to our God," Freneau reminded his readers at a moment of bitter political conflicts in the new American government, "the *sovereignty* still resides with THE PEOPLE, and . . . neither proclamations, nor *royal demeanor and state* can prevent them from exercising it." France's Revolution thus confirmed for Freneau the wisdom of America's political achievements, and his poems often celebrated the two nations and two revolutions that had rejected Europe's most powerful kings.[13]

Freneau never doubted that the well-lighted torch of American national freedom had shown the way for the revolution in France—the popular political claim that appeared also in Thomas Paine's interpretations of the French Revolution. "One of the great advantages of the American revolution," Paine wrote from England in 1792, "has been, that it led to a discovery of the principles . . . of governments. All the revolutions till then had been worked within the atmosphere of a court, and never on the great floor of a nation." The American experience, by contrast, had shown the central political truth of nations and governments: *"That government is nothing more than a national association acting on the principles of society."* With this truth now firmly established, it was in Paine's view "natural to expect that other revolutions will follow."[14] France's revolutionaries did in fact reiterate claims for national sovereignty and human rights that Americans had asserted in their national revolution, yet the national movement in France ultimately contributed far more directly and decisively to the emergence of other nationalisms in Europe.

Nationalism in the French Revolution

Historians have often argued that the French Revolution made the most influential political contributions to modern nationalist theories and policies. For example, the French created new definitions of national citizenship, established new duties for national military service, developed new state institutions for education, and affirmed the sovereignty of the nation over the traditional sovereign power of the king and church. The political meaning of nationalism thus developed rapidly in France during the 1790s, when French revolutionaries referred constantly to the citizens and institutions of the nation. The term "nationalism," however, did not enter political discourse until an antirevolutionary French priest used this new word in 1798 as part of a polemical attack on all the Revolution's ideas and actions.[15] The revolutionaries themselves talked about patriotism, but their descriptions of a patriotic French national identity may not have been altogether new. Reflecting a recent historical interest in the continuities between old regime France and the Revolution, some historians argue that French national identity had already emerged in the seventeenth and eighteenth centuries among nobles (who claimed to represent France's ancient historical traditions), in the centralizing state bureaucracy, in the Catholic Church, in the expanding French press, and in the official codification of the French language.[16]

This emphasis on continuities, which extends the nineteenth-century arguments of Alexis de Tocqueville, suggests that revolutionary ideas about the nation made sense after 1789 because they repeated familiar claims about the distinctive achievements of French culture and the centralizing aspirations of French kings. Yet France's revolutionary activists also introduced crucial new themes to their narrative of the nation. They sought to create an entirely new political system and political identity in France, thereby moving politics from the royal court at Versailles into the new National Assembly in Paris and more generally into the everyday life of French citizens. This political transformation had radical consequences, as Lynn Hunt has explained, because the new national leaders "acted on the conviction that the regenerated Nation was a new community without precedent in history, and this community was based on an ideal of transparent social and political relations." The nation became in this revolutionary account a political entity that was always moving toward a better future rather than defending an imaginary past. Such movement required constant *political* activity in order to sustain the new political culture of national identity and the new political ideal of citizen participation.[17]

The guiding ideas in this new political culture referred (as in America) to national sovereignty and human rights. These two strands of nationalist thought became part of the Revolution's call for "liberty, equality, fraternity," and they entered into other ideals such as republican virtue, but they were stated most clearly in "The Declaration of the Rights of Man and Citizen." This famous document, which the revolutionary National Assembly approved in August 1789, asserted that "all sovereignty rests essentially in the nation. No body and no individual may exercise authority which does not emanate expressly from the nation." The fundamental principle of national sovereignty made laws an "expression of the general will" and ensured the legal equality of all French citizens. Indeed, the theoretical starting point for every specific law and policy of the nation could be found in Article 1 of the Declaration: "Men are born and remain free and equal in rights."[18] The new sovereign nation would therefore differ from the political order of the traditional French state (in which the king was sovereign) and the legal regulation of the traditional French society (in which laws and obligations applied differently to persons in separate social categories). Although the National Assembly did not always adhere to its own declared principles, the "Declaration of Rights" contributed decisively to a new French nationalism by redefining the sovereignty of the French nation, the source of authority for the French state, and the legal rights of French citizens.

These new definitions of the nation appeared also in the vast production of popular political pamphlets that shaped the rapidly expanding sphere of national political debates. Amid the torrent of new political language, the famous pamphlet by the Abbé Sieyès (1748–1836), "What Is the Third Estate?," stands out as the most influential account of a new French national identity. Much like Paine's *Common Sense* in America, Sieyès's pamphlet argued that it was entirely logical for the French to separate themselves from an outdated subservience to political elites that no longer represented the will or the interests of the nation. Denouncing the French nobility's claim for special privileges on the basis of their special service to the state, Sieyès argued that the commoners of the Third Estate actually performed the essential, productive work of the nation. Unlike the nobility, which had become "foreign to the Nation" because "its mission does not emanate from the people," the Third Estate represented the sovereign identity of France. "The Third Estate therefore contains everything that pertains to the Nation," Sieyès wrote, "and nobody outside of the Third Estate can claim to be part of the Nation. What is the Third Estate? EVERYTHING." But this "nation" of the third estate understood the equality of human rights as well as its own essential sovereignty, so within this nation, Sieyès argued, all citizens "are equally dependent on the law, all present it with their liberty and their property to be protected; and this is what I call the *common rights* of citizens, by which they are all alike."[19] Theoretical equality before the law did not mean for Sieyès that all citizens should have

The Triumph of the French Republic under the Auspices of Liberty. Pen and ink with watercolor and gouache, by anonymous artist, c. 1793. Ackland Art Museum, The University of North Carolina, Chapel Hill, Ackland Fund.

The revolutionaries in France believed that they were overturning all the oppressive institutions of human history. This attitude appears clearly in this image of the Republic (the seated woman whose arm embraces liberty) and the heroic action of Hercules (standing with his club). Monarchy and church lie subdued on the ground, the "rights of man" are inscribed on a tablet, and the crowned heads of Europe flee in despair.

equal rights to participate in public life. He strongly supported political distinctions that separated the rights of well-to-do, well-educated "active" citizens from the rights of poor, less-educated "passive" citizens—and separated the political rights of men from the legal rights of women. (Similar distinctions also appeared in American nationalism, including even more radical distinctions between masters and slaves.) Yet such inequalities in political rights did not displace the most fundamental distinctions in Sieyès's account of a true nation: the difference between a national sovereignty based on the people instead of a king and the difference between rights based on national citizenship instead of social class.

Sieyès's dichotomies expressed the evolving themes of a new French national identity, which emerged through an endless account of the differences between the new French nation and an old regime of privilege, hierarchy, and superstition. Seeking to demonstrate the new regime's radical opposition to its political and social predecessor, French revolutionaries proclaimed a new calendar in which "Year One" coincided with the creation of the French Republic (1792). The decree that announced the new calendar described the Revolution's definitive break with all previous history in metaphors that could be compared to early Christian accounts (or dating) of the world before and after Christ. "The French nation, oppressed, degraded during many centuries by the most insolent despotism, has finally awakened to a consciousness of its rights and of the power to which its destinies summon it." To make sure that French citizens remained "awake" to their national rights, however, revolutionary leaders emphasized every possible differentiation from the hated past, including the reorganization of time itself. "It wishes its regeneration to be complete," the official decree on the calendar continued, "in order that its years of liberty and glory may betoken still more by their duration in the history of peoples than its years of slavery and humiliation in the history of kings."[20] It would nevertheless take more than a new calendar to produce the new nation. In fact, the Revolution generated new clothing, new language, new flags, new festivals, new armies, and new institutions, all of which theoretically opposed the old regime and carried the meaning of the new nation into daily life.

Condemnations of the old regime thus reached into every sphere of public and private life, but they failed to produce national unity or the final victory of liberty and equality. Opponents of the Revolution could still be found in all parts of France and along every French frontier, so that successive revolutionary governments waged almost constant warfare after 1792. The revolutionary wars promoted a vivid sense of French national identity as the dominant political narratives extended the attacks against the old regime at home into attacks against oppressive old regimes abroad. A declaration of war on Prussia and Austria in 1792, for example, offered an occasion for the National Assembly to explain the meaning of its conflicts in a general proclamation to the people of France and the kings of Europe. "The French nation is free, and . . . conscious of its liberty. It is free; it is armed; it cannot be enslaved." This freedom had to be defended, however, in military campaigns that pitted "the just defence of a free people against the unjust aggression of a king." Repeating the themes of America's earlier separation from Britain and anticipating the rationale for most modern national wars, the French described their war as the necessary response to the provocations of an enemy with whom it was impossible to compromise. "To arms!" began a Jacobin proclamation in the following year. "The terrible hour is at hand when the defenders of the *Patrie* must vanquish or bury themselves under the bloody ruins of the Republic. Frenchmen, never was your liberty in such great peril!"[21]

War was thus portrayed as a consequence of the national support for sovereignty and human rights, and the requisite sacrifices were justified through the stark opposition of freedom and slavery. In the words of the popular revolutionary "Chant du départ," French soldiers fought the forces of absolute despotism: "Tremble, enemies of France, / Kings drunk with blood and pride, / The Sovereign people advance, / Tyrants, descend into the Grave!"[22] Such narratives about royal enemies and the sovereign French nation translated the abstractions of political oratory into a comprehensible story for even the most illiterate soldier.

The political definition of warfare described a national campaign on behalf of shared political ideals and brought all citizens into the service of a fully mobilized nation. Faced with enemies and defeats on all fronts, the revolutionary government decreed its famous *Levée en masse* in August 1793, thereby defining the duties of everyone in France and setting an example for the total wars of all modern nations.

> The young men shall go to battle; the married men shall
> forge arms and transport provisions; the women shall make
> tents and clothes, and shall serve in the hospitals; the chil-

dren shall turn old linen into lint; the old men shall repair to the public places, to stimulate the courage of the warriors and preach the unity of the Republic and hatred of kings.[23]

This national call to arms proved successful in saving the Revolution from its domestic and foreign enemies, but its significance carried far beyond specific battles of the 1790s. France had demonstrated how a new national government could mobilize its population and material resources with coercion *and* ideology. Young men often joined the French army as conscripts, yet they were constantly told that they fought for universal political principles (sovereignty of the nation, freedom, equality) as well as the defense of their national territory. Like the Americans before them, French political activists believed their Revolution carried universal rather than local significance, and they confidently assumed their own nation's victories would promote freedom and equality in every European state.

The political theories of the French Revolution thus spread rapidly across Europe, but the diffusion of such ideas required far more than successful military campaigns. New claims for national sovereignty, human rights, and legal reforms could only develop and spread in the language and symbols of a new political discourse, which the French mobilized earlier and even more effectively than they mobilized their armies. Political nationalism needed new images and narratives in order to define the nation's identity and to change both the French social order and the wider world of European politics. This social and political reconstruction could not possibly proceed without the reconstruction of symbols and languages that had long sustained the old regime church and monarchy. In short, as Rousseau had argued in *The Social Contract,* a new republican nation must have a new civil religion. Political abstractions such as "natural rights" could not match the traditional aura of a king or the rituals of a Catholic mass in generating emotional attachments and personal loyalties to the state. Revolutionary leaders therefore developed alternative rituals to bring the new nation's political themes into the various spheres of everyday life. They promoted a new national identity through festivals, monuments, artwork, plays, "liberty trees," liberty caps and clothing, tricolor cockades, and countless other symbols of a regenerated French nation. The saints of Catholicism gave way to national martyrs, and the traditional images of St. Mary or the royal family gave way to the new goddess of liberty, Marianne. Statues of Marianne or Hercules offered illiterate persons the visual imagery to understand that national liberty and equality had replaced the king and church at the symbolic center of French life. Lacking a George Washington to serve as the symbol of political unity, the French represented the nation's identity and political meaning in portraits, festivals, and statues of "Liberty" and the "Republic."[24]

Revolutionary festivals, for example, were designed to provide a continuing political education for people who had to learn the new national catechism in much the same way that people learned how to be religious. The moral purpose of national festivals, wrote one of their advocates, was to give individual citizens a lifelong emotional connection to France by showing them how the bonds of a nation resembled the most intimate personal attachments in a family. The nation should be "the mother of all citizens, who gives them all the same milk, who brings them up and treats them as brothers and who, by the care that she lavishes equally upon all, gives them that air of family resemblance that distinguishes a people brought up in this way from all the other peoples of the earth. . . . She takes hold of the man and never leaves him, so that the upbringing of the nation is an institution not only for childhood, but for the whole life."[25] Political education and public rituals thus taught people to believe that their lives could not be separated from the life of a nation. In other words, a person without a nation was like a person without a family.

This narrative of national identity was repeated constantly in visual icons, literature, poems, and songs. The songwriter François de Neufchâteau, for example, wrote a "Hymn to Liberty" that transformed traditional injunctions to serve God into new political commands to serve the nation: "Love one's country and one's brothers, / Serve the sovereign people, / These are the sacred characteristics, / And the faith of a Republican."[26] The story of national allegiance in Neufchâteau's "Hymn" and in other songs such as Rouget de Lisle's "Marsaillaise" offered visions of national unity and freedom that could never be completely fulfilled. This frustrated desire for a unified nation contributed to the violence and systematic Terror of the Revolution. More generally, narratives of political inclusion and equality within the nation also *excluded* groups (for example, women) who were placed outside the nation's public life.

Yet the revolutionary narratives about "liberty, equality, fraternity" also created a new national identity for which large numbers of French people were willing to kill or die. Although the Terror and the subsequent imperialism of French armies discredited many of the

Oath of the Federation of 14 July 1790. Etching and aquatint by Le Coeur, after Swebach, 1790. Division of Rare and Manuscript Collections, Carl A. Kroch Library, Cornell University.

All nationalisms use festivals and holidays to foster national identities. The first anniversary of the fall of the Bastille prison during the French Revolution was celebrated with a new nationalist ritual that has remained important for every subsequent French republic. Note the various classes, professions, ages, and genders that are represented in this festival of national unity.

Revolution's political theories, the national theme of fraternity continued to flourish in the Napoleonic French state after 1799. It also began to appear among the European critics of France's national power. Indeed, the expansive nationalism in France gradually helped to create its most dangerous rivals by stimulating anti-French nationalisms throughout Europe. No matter what they thought of "liberty" and "equality," Europeans could find ideals for their own states and cultures in the revolutionary concept of national "fraternity."

National Responses to the French Revolution

French revolutionaries proclaimed the rights of national liberty and self-determination, but their military campaigns in the late 1790s increasingly denied these rights to other European societies. The French thus contributed a positive ideology (self-determination) to justify resistance to their own policies (conquest) and helped to produce a new self-consciousness about national identities throughout much of Europe. Within France itself, the revolutionary themes of national citizenship and political participation evolved into a Bonapartist nationalism that demanded service to the sovereign nation-state but dispensed with the human rights that had been so important to the earlier, liberal view of the nation.[27] Yet Napoleon and his emissaries claimed to bring the universal principles of Enlightenment reason and reform to the countries that fell under French control, thus creating a political context in which the opposition to French imperialism could easily merge with a cultural critique of "French" Enlightenment theories. There were of course conservative strands in French nationalism (as Napoleon demonstrated in many of his own policies), but for most persons outside France the critique of revolutionary and imperial France became also a critique of the liberal Enlightenment.

This conservative critique developed in both the British and German responses to the French Revolution. Although most British and German intellectuals strongly supported the early liberal reforms of the French Revolution, the subsequent Terror and military expansion rapidly eroded this early identification with France and helped to produce new ideologies that celebrated the unique value of British and German national traditions. British nationalists, for example, defined their national mission in defiant anti-French language (as one popular ballad put it, "God smash the French . . . , We'll shoot them every one"), but the national mobilization of British soldiers may also have contributed to a more democratic British society. The

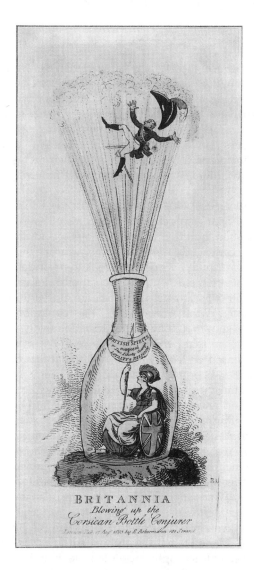

Britannia Blowing Up the Corsican Bottle Conjurer. Etching with hand coloring by an unknown artist, published by R. Ackermann, 1803. From the copy in the Rare Book Collection, The University of North Carolina, Chapel Hill.

Wars against the French Revolution and Napoleon strengthened nationalist attitudes among all social classes in Britain. This image of Napoleon's unhappy fate shows the consequences of "British Spirits," which are "composed of True Liberty, Courage, Loyalty & Religion."

anti-French struggle acquired some of the traits of a Jacobin *levée en masse*, and common soldiers who joined the national campaign would have new grounds for demanding and expecting more political participation in the post-war British state.[28] The French enemy was therefore both rejected and (in some respects) imitated during the long wars with revolutionary and Napoleonic France. For the most part, however, British ideological responses to the French Revolution and Napoleon pushed the evolving British nationalism toward conservative ideas about Britain's distinctive political and social institutions.

This newly defined British nationalism stressed national differences from the threatening new regime of the French Revolution, a theme that shaped both the theory and passion of Edmund Burke's (1729–1797) famous *Reflections on the Revolution in France* (1790). Burke's book became a founding text of modern conservatism, but it also provided the narrative for a new nationalism that defined the meaning of Britain through its opposition to the French Revolution and the political theories of the French Enlightenment. In contrast to the French, Burke wrote, the English were happy "to derive all we possess as *an inheritance from our forefathers.*" Whereas the French blindly embraced reason, radicalism, and revolution, the English nation honored the wisdom of its ancestors and protected its historical legacy in the continuity of its traditional institutions. Comparing the English to a cud-chewing cow in the shadow of a "British oak," Burke assumed (or hoped) that England would never accept political ideas from France. "Thanks to our sullen resistance to innovation, thanks to the cold sluggishness of our national character, we still bear the stamp of our forefathers. . . . We are not the converts of Rousseau; we are not the disciples of Voltaire." More precisely, Burke continued, "we are generally men of untaught feelings, . . . [and] instead of casting away all our old prejudices, we cherish them to a very considerable degree, . . . and the longer they have lasted and the more generally they have prevailed, the more we cherish them."[29] In short, Burke's critique of the French Revolution developed the intellectual rationale for a new British nationalism that was hostile to Enlightenment universalism and rationalist confidence in radical reforms—but filled with praise and warm "feelings" for the distinctiveness and mysteries of a specific national culture.

Burke's writings later attracted sympathetic readers in Germany, where an interest in the specificity of national cultures had already emerged in the work of Johann Gottfried von Herder (1744–1803) and other intellectuals who challenged various Enlightenment claims for the transcultural truths of reason. In contrast to Burke, however, most German intellectuals at first welcomed the French Revolution because it represented what Friedrich von Gentz (1764–1832) called "the first practical triumph of philosophy, [and] the first example of a form of government founded upon principles and upon an integrated consistent system of thought." Gentz soon became a bitter critic of the Revolution, but he was still praising the French in late 1790 for their assaults on the "many ancient evils" of tyranny and oppressive governments.[30]

Such views were by no means unusual among the many intellectuals who believed that the Revolution offered philosophical and political lessons for Germany. A revolutionary republic was actually established at Mainz in the German Rhineland (October 1792), giving at least some German political activists reason to believe that a new era of international freedom and equality had begun.[31] Although the short-lived republicanism in Mainz did not inspire other Jacobin experiments in Germany, many Germans continued to admire France during the later revolutionary and Napoleonic wars, in part because the French showed how a unified, mobilized nation could enact reforms, protect its own territory, and also impose its political will on others. Prominent figures such as Wilhelm von Humboldt (reformer of Prussian education and the university system) drew on French ideas as they set about modernizing the Prussian state. Meanwhile, some of the most creative thinkers in Germany—including Goethe and Hegel—never embraced the nationalist critique of France or Napoleon. Early-nineteenth-century German nationalism often promoted liberal ideas such as national sovereignty and human rights, and liberal nationalists called for reforms to change the prevailing privileges, organization, and rationale of the diverse German states.[32]

Despite the liberal political strands in German culture, however, a much stronger intellectual-political movement vehemently condemned the French Revolution and developed a new account (mostly after 1800) of how German culture differed profoundly from the French. Friedrich von Gentz, whose transition from supporter to angry critic exemplified the changing German view of France, translated Burke's *Reflections* into German (1793) and began publishing his own dire warnings about the dangers of France's entire revolutionary project. Gentz decided that Germans could learn nothing from the French example except that such revolutions led to disastrous outcomes. "The French Revolution never had a definite object," Gentz wrote in 1800, so it "ran through the unbounded space of a fantastic arbitrary will, and of a bottomless anarchy." Denying the most basic human feelings and needs, the Revolution could "only force its way by violence and crimes," all of which Germany must reject in order to protect its own institutions and society.[33] A new generation of intellectuals thus moved (like Gentz) beyond the politics of the French Revolution to develop a new definition of the nation, stressing German differences from France and the Enlightenment. Although this emphasis on difference resembled the themes of Burke's work in England, German writers tended to emphasize their nation's distinctive culture, *Volk*, and philosophical insights more than their unique political institutions. Herder's earlier writings on the diversity of national cultures, for example, offered an attractive theory for explaining why German culture could and should survive after Napoleon's crushing defeat of the Prussian and Austrian armies in 1806. This was the military-political context for Fichte's *Addresses to the German Nation*, which argued that Germans must come together "into a single close-connected force" in order to regenerate the nation and promote the "unity and concord" of Germany's national spirit.[34]

The new philosophical appeals to the German nation did not address specific questions of political or military reform, but they clarified the cultural meaning of Germany by emphasizing the German difference from France. Opposition to French politics and culture enabled German nationalists to describe what it meant to be German, no matter how much individual German states or persons may differ among themselves. "Let the unanimity of your hearts be your church," wrote the poet Ernst Moritz Arndt (1769–1860) in 1814, "let hatred of the French be your religion, let Freedom and Fatherland be your saints, to whom you pray." Calls for German unity thus emerged from the constantly invoked dangers of a French enemy whose differences posed the starkest dangers to Germany's national existence. "France has become for us the true antithesis in the struggle in which all our moral forces are called forth," the journalist Joseph Görres (1776–1848) explained in a concise summary of the identity-shaping oppositions of the era; "it is a center of devouring fire and the totality of all evil, . . . and the struggle with it will . . . force the missing unity upon our people and thus avert us from civil war."[35]

The immediate object of such declarations was of course the military defeat of Napoleon, but the larger enemy in this campaign for the German nation could be found in the political ideas and policies of France's Enlightenment and Revolution. Defined as an alien imposition on German culture, French ideas became an all-important object for critique in the construction of German nationalism. These nation-shaping interactions between France and Germany continued long after the Napoleonic era, though the interactions did not simply depend on or sustain ideas of national difference. Nationalists in each society also drew on the other to develop new accounts or definitions of their own national cultures. There would always be Germans who invoked the French Enlightenment and liberal political ideas as alternatives to the cultural or philosophical themes of German nationalism, and French nationalists in later eras would draw on German ideas about the uniqueness of cultures and national populations to describe their own distinctive language, traditions, and *peuple*. The nationalism of the French Revolution therefore helped generate new nationalisms in England and Germany. These other nationalisms, in turn, helped extend and redefine nationalism in France, and European political culture has carried the nationalist legacy of the revolutionary era into all its later warfare, economic rivalries, and political disputes.

The Nationalist Political Legacy of the American and French Revolutions

The nearly universal modern belief that every nation must have its own state and that each state must represent a sovereign nation constantly reiterates key political themes of the eighteenth-century revolutions in America and Europe. From that era until the present, national movements have claimed to express the sovereign political will of specific national populations and to defend the human rights of freedom and political equality. The American and French Revolutions embodied for contemporaries and for later interpreters the political ideas and institutions of liberal nationalism. Although the ideas were repeatedly violated in both societies (for example, in America's treatment of Indians and slaves and in France's imperialist wars and repression of dissent), *theories* of national sovereignty and human rights shaped both the American Declaration of Independence and the French Declaration of the Rights of Man and Citizen. More generally, such theories often reappeared in later national movements throughout Europe, South America, Asia, and Africa, all of which produced political narratives to describe their nations and the political principles of their national cultures.

Yet the narratives that create national political identities have always described the nation with explicit or implicit references to other (past or present) nations that differ from and oppose the ideals of the nationalists. Definitions of difference appeared as frequently as the claims for political rights in national narratives because the imagined community requires outsiders or enemies in order to define the imagined unity and coherence of the nation. Liberal nationalists, for example, defined their revolutionary national objectives in opposition to Old World Monarchs and corrupt old regimes, whereas the new conservative nationalists defined their theories in opposition to republican revolutions and Enlightenment intellectuals.

Later nationalisms often developed a much stronger emphasis on differences of race, ethnicity, religion, or language, but even the most militant cultural nationalisms usually asserted theories of political sovereignty that had appeared earlier in America's Declaration of Independence. Equally important, all modern nationalisms have resembled the French Revolution in their use of rituals, festivals, icons, and monuments to construct and narrate the meaning of the nation. Among the many political consequences of the American and French Revolutions, the contributions to nationalist theory and practice may well be the most enduring and influential. Nationalist ideals and institutions have obviously differed enormously in various historical contexts, yet every modern nationalism has developed a political theory of sovereign rights, a narrative of national differences, and a language of national symbols.

3

Nationalism, Language, and Writing

All nations and nationalisms must have languages to represent their political and cultural identities, but this link between nationalisms and languages carries significantly different meanings for most nationalists and cultural historians. Nationalists typically claim that languages express essential national, cultural identities and that distinctive linguistic cultures should have their own nation-states. Cultural historians also emphasize the importance of language, yet they tend to reject essentialist cultural and linguistic accounts of the nation. According to most cultural historians, nationalists have constructed the symbols and narratives of nations to create social coherence within specific territories and to justify the modern exercise of political power. Where the nationalist sees a deep linguistic spirit emerging in modern nation-states, the cultural historian is likely to see modern nationalist institutions and states retrospectively constructing the cultural and linguistic coherence that past generations never recognized or understood. For the advocates of both arguments, however, language and writing generate the dynamic, evolving identity of nations and nationalisms.

Although historians often draw strong distinctions between cultural nationalisms (emphasis on language and ethnicity) and political nationalisms (emphasis on political rights), this description of differences can obscure the crucial linguistic traits that all nationalisms share. In addition to the obvious need for linguistic symbols and rituals, virtually all nationalisms advocate and celebrate a single, unifying language. Praise for the unique qualities of the English and French languages, for example, became an important early theme in the political nationalisms of England and France. It would therefore be wrong to assume that writers in central and eastern Europe were the only nationalists to justify their aspirations for political unity and independence on the basis of linguistic traditions. Many of the most notable *linguistic* explanations for national autonomy and identity nevertheless emerged first in central Europe, where authors such as Herder and Fichte argued that different cultural assumptions were embedded in different languages. "Every nation," wrote Herder, "is one people, having its own national form, as well as *its own language*." Herder did not deny that deep similarities could be found among people in various national cultures, but his emphasis on the intricate overlap of language and ideas contributed the linguistic insights that others extended into nationalist political theories. When people speak different languages, nationalists would argue, they express different ideas and develop different institutions—all of which should be embodied in the governments of different nation-states. As Fichte summarized the argument, "wherever a separate language is found, there a separate nation exists, which has the right to take independent charge of its affairs and to govern itself."[1]

Nationalists therefore assumed that language both expressed and protected the life of a nation, and the loss of language would cause its death. Expanding these linguistic assumptions to the battlefield, nationalists linked the battle against French armies to the national resistance against the French language. "When a nation's language falls into disrepute and decay," wrote one German patriot shortly after the Napoleonic wars, ". . . the manner in which it observes and judges things is also lost." The French threat to the German language was thus equivalent to France's destruction of the Prussian army because suppression of the language destroyed the essential, unifying bond of the German people.[2] Anti-Napoleonic nationalism in Germany pointed to linguistic identity as the foundation for national political institutions and thus developed an intellectual rationale for subsequent national movements in all parts of the world. New nations evolved (in this view) from old languages into social and political alliances that culminated in new political states. "Those who speak the same language," Fichte explained, "are joined to each other by a multitude of invisible bonds by nature herself, long before any human art begins; . . . they belong together and are by nature one and inseparable."[3]

Fichte's account of how language created natural "invisible bonds" expressed a common nationalist view of the nation's essential cultural identity. For most contemporary cultural historians, however, the arguments of Fichte and other like-minded authors suggest how the nation is actually constructed or imagined by those who claim to speak for the "people,"—a vague but apparently unified collectivity that becomes coherent in the rhetoric of nationalist philosophers and political leaders. People live in specific places, of course, and they speak specific languages, but they do not become a nation until they are defined as a national community in the writings of a nationalist movement.

Nations were "written" into a new cultural prominence and identity through the new linguistic and historical studies of early-nineteenth-century authors. At the same time, these new narratives increasingly entered the lives of literate people through new schools and other state institutions that spread cultural and political descriptions of the nation to communities that had rarely or never imagined themselves as part of a large national state. People in such scattered places did not naturally become French or German or Russian or any other national identity, but they learned to describe themselves with such adjectives as they attended schools, public festivals, church services, or military ceremonies and as they read new books and newspapers. The political and literary cultures of nations were thus shaped through countless communicative acts that gradually extended nationalist ideas and practices into almost every aspect of daily life.[4]

New forms of literature and history reported the distinctive national sacrifices of previous generations and explained how national heroes had served the universal progress of humanity as well as the specific interests of the nation. Adjusted to fit the circumstances of each nation, the themes of personal sacrifice and collective purpose became familiar in all the Romantic nationalisms of the early nineteenth century. Philosophers, poets, novelists, and historians narrated the cultural meaning of the nation in writings that went far beyond the official declarations or policies of political leaders, and yet the literary works often replicated the most straightforward political and military dichotomies of national difference. The language of the nation had to be defended against other languages and cultures that flourished like other national enemies inside and outside the nation. The dangers and differences called for strong action, but the nation's cultural identity also depended on the continued existence of such dangers, because national meaning and purpose emerged most clearly in the opposition to other people and cultures.

The revolutionary activists in France, for example, defined their national language against both the hierarchical language of the old regime and the regional patois languages that seemed to threaten the political unity and cultural coherence of the nation. Local dialects represented a linguistic difference that could easily fuse with political differences to undermine the national revolution. As the Abbé Grégoire (1750–1831) stressed in a report to the National Convention (1794), "On the necessity and the methods for destroying the Patois and making usage of the French language universal," the "universalizing" political aspirations of the Revolution could only be accomplished in a shared French language. The new political nationalism in France linked political reforms to linguistic reforms and described French culture with recurring references to cultural and linguistic differences.[5]

Critics of the Revolution and the subsequent imperial expansion also seized on the linguistic meaning of French politics, so that the attack on revolutionary ideas often overlapped with a wider cultural attack on the French language. German nationalists argued that French was a weak language whose derivation from the ancient Latin precluded the originality and creative strength of German. A strong, original nation, in this linguistic view, could only emerge from an original language. Much like the political dichotomies in French linguistic theory (national or republican versus local or monarchical), the description of national culture in Germany presumed a linguistic difference (original versus derivative) that gave German a higher position in the national cultural hierarchy. "It is only a daughter language," noted a typical German commentary on the derivative, gendered weakness of French, "a spurious language, deflected and subjected by tyrants." Language therefore produced and reflected the essential traits of a nation, including its creativity, originality, and even its national virility. The best language, according to German theorists, emerged from the depths of the national population, whereas weaker languages evolved out of other cultures and the contrivances of academic elites. "Naturalness on the German side," Fichte explained in his summary of the linguistic dichotomy, "arbitrariness and artificiality on the foreign side."[6]

Similar claims for cultural superiority could extend to the literature of a nation as well as its language, though the status of national literatures was typically established, like the status of languages, through comparisons with other cultures and a strong desire for cultural purity. The Polish poet Adam Mickiewicz (1798–1855), for example, asserted the superiority of a Slavic literature that grew directly out of "the soul of the people," thereby sustaining a unique literary culture that "differed completely" from the writers and books of other nations.[7] The problem for such linguistic and literary advocates of the nation, however, resembled the problem facing the political advocates of nationalism. Nationalist narratives described a unified, pure national language, yet the meaning of this linguistic identity depended on its relation to other languages that threatened both the purity and the ideas of the true national language. Given these problems of linguistic interaction and infiltration, national narratives about linguistic and cultural identity had to be constantly promoted and rewritten in nationalist publications, songs, art, and schools. The "people," in other words, had to learn how they were connected and why they were a nation.

Spreading the Language of the Nation

The nationalist belief in popular, national, unifying languages faced the disconcerting reality of linguistic diversity in every would-be national society. There were at least 30 regional patois languages in France, for example, and incomprehensible differences between the rural and urban languages in Germany. The call for national political and cultural unity was therefore stymied in practice by the fact that much of the "national" population could not understand what their national leaders said on their behalf. "The people," explained the French reformer Grégoire, "must understand the laws to approve and obey them."[8] Grégoire wanted to create a new republican nation, but he realized like most of his revolutionary allies that this new nation could not exist until the people of France shared a common language. He therefore developed ambitious proposals to diffuse a standardized republican French language into the villages of France, emphasizing the need for new schools and grammar books. The French nation was to be reformed through education, which meant that the French political revolution became also a prolonged campaign for educational reforms.

This new nationalization of the masses might be compared to earlier conversions of European populations to Christianity. "Missionaries" went into the countryside to establish new schools, teach the alien national language, and combat older beliefs and sources of local identity. The language of elites had to be translated into the language of common people (and vice versa), though in theory the teachers were returning the national language to a population from which it had come. "We must popularize the language," wrote the French linguistic activist Barère, "we must destroy this aristocracy of language that seems to establish a polite nation in the middle of a barbarous nation. We have revolutionized the government . . . [and] we must now also revolutionize the language."[9]

Education thus became an early and enduring concern of France's successive revolutionary governments, but (as in so many other aspects of modern nationalism) the Revolution's foreign critics also endorsed many of the French-style reforms in their own societies. Every nationalist movement wanted to revolutionize and nationalize education. Fichte's *Addresses to the German Nation* gave more attention to the need for a "new education" than to any other issue in German culture and society, because education offered the specific institutional structure for national survival and regeneration. "By means of the new education," Fichte argued, "we want to mould the Germans into a corporate body, which shall be stimulated and animated in all its individual members by the same interest."[10] Utopian aspirations for national unity thus generated utopian proposals for teaching the German population how it might actually acquire the linguistic and philosophical qualities of the ideal German nation. But the Germans were by no means alone in looking to education for their national unity and salvation. "Without National Education," the exiled Italian nationalist Joseph Mazzini (1805–1872) wrote in the 1830s, ". . . a nation has no moral existence."[11]

The influence of nationalist plans for changing national education varied widely, depending of course on the relation between nationalist writers and the governments in their societies. An exiled Italian or Polish nationalist had less direct impact on education policies than, say, the intellectuals who worked for the French government. Even the most active intellectual intervention could not produce the national morality and unity that nationalists envisioned, but schools did become increasingly important in the creation of new national identities. The French government's expenditure on education, for example, roughly quadrupled between 1789 and 1812. New textbooks taught national languages and national histories, new maps provided the visual imagery for students to place themselves within national boundaries, and new school examinations defined the shared national knowledge as well as the people who could get jobs in the national government and national economy. Education moved steadily from the churches into the hands of state bureaucracies, which opened the schools to far more people (at least at the elementary level). Educated workers and soldiers were needed in new national economies and armies, where the citizens of nineteenth-century nations continued to learn about their national states and cultures long after they had left their schools. Young persons who entered national business enterprises or national military units quickly recognized that advancement in every sphere required knowledge of the national language, culture, and government. Elite national languages thus challenged and gradually displaced local vernacular languages, partly in the schools and partly in the other institutions of modernizing European states. Children learned and were rewarded for their national identities in schools, but they also relearned and were rewarded for their national identities throughout their later lives.[12]

The collective activities of education, state bureaucracies, and national economic institutions all depended on written information and ideas, a universal pattern that connects the history of nationalism to the modern history of publishing and journalism and mass communications. Some historians have in fact described the modern nation as a centralized communications network that carries national narratives of events and culture from major urban centers into all classes and geographical regions of a political state. Modern nationalism (in this view) entered public life through the newspapers and publications industry that emerged before and after the eighteenth-century political revolutions. New books, pamphlets, journals, maps, and newspapers flowed from the printing presses of nations and nationalist movements, giving people the language to locate themselves in national territories and collective national stories. Literacy created a booming market for publishers, so that new nationalisms developed at the intersection of education, communications, and the new economy. As Benedict Anderson has argued in his account of this historical transition, "the convergence of capitalism and print technology on the fatal diversity of human language created the possibility of a new form of imagined community."[13] Daily newspapers brought the nation into the lives of individuals who had learned to read the national story at school, and national rituals (as reported in newspapers) provided continuities and meanings that had once come from the rituals, calendars, and bells of the church.

The rapid expansion of education, book publishing, journalism, and other forms of national communication created the need for a growing number of writers to produce the new narratives of the nation. Schools needed textbooks, language manuals, examinations, and teachers; newspapers needed journalists; publishing houses needed authors; and all nationalist movements and governments needed literary advocates. In short, a new class of intellectual experts and critics emerged with the new nationalisms and demanded a special status within the state (or in exile) as defenders of the "people," the literature, and the history of a national community. "The noblest privilege and the most sacred function of the man of letters," wrote Fichte, "is . . . to assemble his nation and to take counsel with it about

Crossing the Bridge at Arcole. Etching and engraving by Fiayn and Chaponnier, after a drawing by Lembert, c. 1797. From the copy in the Rare Book Collection, The University of North Carolina, Chapel Hill.

Telling the story of the nation required art as well as history books and newspapers. This engraving depicts a famous event in the wars of the French Republic during the late 1790s and suggests the heroic national service that French citizens should emulate. A young Napoleon bravely leads his troops to victory in Italy beneath flags that represent the "French People" and "French Republic."

its most important affairs." Writers could contribute even more than governments to the life of nations, particularly when they claimed—to quote Fichte again—that the nation "was held together as a common whole almost solely by the . . . man of letters, by speech and writing."[14] This argument for the significance of writers was of course a flattering self-referential view of how literature defined national life, but it was also at least partially accurate inasmuch as the nation took its imagined coherence from the narratives of its history and ideas and enemies. The need for writers was as great as the need for soldiers. In fact, it would be impossible in this respect to separate political nationalisms from cultural nationalisms. Writers and their national texts defined every national identity, though the status and themes of writers who sought the creation of new nation-states often differed from the status and themes of writers who represented the nationalisms of established nation-states.

Fichte's description of writers gave them exceptional importance to the nation, but his views were not unusual. From the other side of the Atlantic, for example, Ralph Waldo Emerson (1803–1882) was urging American writers to add their work to the new American nation's struggle for national independence. Calling for a new American culture in his famous essay "The American Scholar" (1837), Emerson described the scholar as a "man who must take up into himself all the ability of the time, all the contributions of the past, all the hopes of the future." This project required writing and thinking that could break free from the national cultures of Europe and produce new narratives for the New World. "We have listened too long to the courtly muses of Europe," he complained in the essay that went on to describe what the writers of a new nation must do. "We will walk on our own feet; we will work with our own hands; we will speak our own minds. The study of letters shall be no longer a name for pity, for doubt, and for sensual indulgence." Instead, Emerson continued, the scholar (who was always male in this description) would provide the practical service of linking individuals to a higher world of national and spiritual transcendence. "A nation of men will for the first time exist, because each believes himself inspired by the Divine Soul which also inspires all men."[15]

Despite the differences between Fichte's faith in the national spirit and Emerson's faith in individualism, both authors wrote narratives of national identity that circulated in schools, books, and newspapers. They both lectured to university audiences, published their lectures for wider public audiences, and became public symbols of their national cultures. The diffusion of nationalist ideas in such writings suggests the influence of intellectuals in modern national movements—an influence that resembles the role of theologians and clergy in the diffusion of religions. Yet the self-conscious advocates of the nation could not simply proclaim the nation's existence in the language and independence of its people. They had to show long-term continuities in the national literatures, religions, politics, and histories that *separated* their nations from other cultures and *connected* their nations to the past as well as to the spirit of their own era.

National Literatures and National Identities

The search for the distinctive traits of national cultures raised questions about where the meaning of such cultures could be clearly identified. Although nationalists commonly referred to the "people," it was difficult to describe the specific qualities or ideas that gave diverse, anonymous populations their shared national identity. The history of writing and linguistic usage therefore provided some of the best evidence for the belief in coherent national cultures, because literary works were interpreted as expressions of the national spirit and ideals. An earlier Enlightenment desire to write about universal reason and general truths gave way in many places to a new Romantic emphasis on the particular truths and national experiences that appeared in specific national literatures. Romantic literature thus overlapped with Romantic nationalism throughout much of Europe and America, linking the Romantic literary belief in unique creative artists with the Romantic nationalist belief in unique creative cultures. The Romantic literary critique of the Enlightenment could be found in all parts of the Western world, but many historians stress the exceptional appeal of Romanticism for German intellectuals who resented their marginal position within both the fragmented German states and the wider intellectual networks of Europe. Critics of German nationalism have argued that unhappy writers celebrated their own national literature and language in order to establish their own social status, to resist the universalizing claims of the Enlightenment, and to assert their independence from the political legacy of the French Revolution.[16] The argument for German intellectual *ressentiment* relies on debatable generalities, but the connections between Romanticism and nationalism were extremely important in Germany and other central European societies. More generally, however, Romantic writers in all modern cultures argued that literature embodied the truth of the nation.

National writing took many different forms in early-nineteenth-century literary cultures, including novels, dramas, literary criticism, philosophy, poetry, and history. Popular novelists such as Sir Walter Scott and James Fenimore Cooper wrote about the past and created national literary characters whom readers came to know like the national political characters in their newspapers. Benefiting from the growth of the publishing industry and the expanding market of readers, novelists described national heroes or traditions and often linked love of the nation to other forms of love in families and personal life. Readers learned from novels how to follow the stories of characters whose ideals, sacrifices, conflicts, and separations expressed the themes of wider national cultures. The imagined world of the novel helped people imagine the world of their nation, because novels were filled (like newspapers) with accounts of different persons acting at the same time in a shared space and national story. Novels thus told the stories of nations, and nations were narrated like the stories in novels.[17]

The rise of the novel helped spawn new forms of literary criticism that evaluated and interpreted the national literature for a growing public audience. Prominent critics such as Charles Augustin Sainte-Beuve (1804–1869) in France and William Hazlitt (1778–1830) in Britain described their national cultures in newspaper commentaries on canonical literary figures (e.g., Molière and Shakespeare) and in critical reviews of works by new national writers. Literary criticism thus became part of the national story and national memory. Meanwhile, a new generation of scholars extended their research from literary history into the deeper, obscure history of language itself. Philology became a major branch of academic research through the work of linguists such as Jacob Grimm (1785–1863), who provided systematic accounts of the grammar and the origins of words in national languages. Grimm's own philological research carried strong nationalist and political connotations because he assumed (like many of his academic colleagues in Germany) that the German language expressed a deep national unity. Linguistic researchers thus joined with novelists and literary critics in producing stories of long-developing, essential national identities, though the philologists sometimes went beyond their literary compatriots in trying to identify the pure linguistic traits that separated their nation from foreign cultures and traditions.[18] Despite the often arcane themes of linguistic research, the study of national languages supported and reflected popular assumptions about the linguistic origins of a distinctive national spirit.

Yet the truths of a nation could not be understood until they appeared in the literary forms of philosophy and poetry. Nationalists therefore assumed that philosophers and poets shared a common responsibility to express the national spirit in writings that would give the nation a literary image of itself. This task gave writers an especially important role in the life of nations, but it was a role that philosophers such as Fichte were happy to embrace. Fichte believed that German philosophy enabled the German people to recognize their originality, freedom, morality, and historical destiny. To put it simply (as Fichte rarely did), philosophy gave Germany the knowledge it needed to "make itself wholly and completely what it ought to be." Fichte thus held the most optimistic expectations for his own national philosophy, though he also worried like other nationalists about the deadly foreign influences that were forever threatening the national life of the mind. German philosophy could only flourish when it expressed the creative insights of its own national culture and resisted the derivative ideas of other languages or traditions. Philosophy must draw knowledge from its own national language and then give these national truths back to the people in the language of great poetry. Indeed, "the thinker is himself a poet," Fichte wrote, because living ideas should be communicated in an imaginative living language. "Such a language has within itself the power of infinite poetry, ever refreshing and renewing its youth, for every stirring of living thought in it opens up a new vein of poetic enthusiasm. To such a language, therefore, poetry is the highest and best means of flooding the life of all with the spiritual culture that has been attained."[19] A vital national culture produced poetic philosophers and philosophical poets, all of whom described the spirit and ideals of people who could not describe their own identity so precisely or poetically for themselves.

German writers developed the early systematic argument for this cultural meaning of national identity, but similar themes spread through all the Romantic nationalisms of the era. Adam Mickiewicz, for example, assumed that true philosophers resembled great poets in drawing their wisdom from the distinctive spirit of a nation, and he complained about Polish philosophers who embraced alien German ideas. As for the poets themselves, Mickiewicz argued that the most imaginative were always inspired by the "great life that animates the people" rather than by the lessons they learned in schools. Mickiewicz was of course a poet, so it is not surprising to find him giving poets the cultural importance that Fichte gave to philosophers. No poet, Mickiewicz conceded, could completely describe the past or the future, yet the imaginative poetic writer expressed the needs of the people and *acted* to create a better future for the nation. Poets must sometimes be "dominated by the masses," but they must also strive at other times to push the people toward a higher level of national understanding and action. In every case, however, the poets derived their power "from the vital force of a *nationality*."[20] Great poets, in other words, needed nations just as surely as great nations needed poets.

Mickiewicz lived in Paris as he waged his literary campaign to define a distinctive Polish identity, and he drew constantly on non-Polish sources to describe the nation from which he was permanently exiled. One of his favorite writers was Ralph Waldo Emerson, whose nation was located, like Poland, on the margins of Western Europe and whose vision of an autonomous American culture included a special role for poets. Following the Romantic cultural assumptions of the era, Emerson assumed that the poet "sees and handles that which others dream of" in nature, daily life, and the complexities of language. Unlike Fichte and Mickiewicz, however, he could find no philosopher poet in his own nation to summarize the essential national spirit—though he believed that new nations resembled old nations in needing such voices to describe their meaning. "We have yet had no genius in America," he wrote, who could see "the value of our incomparable materials" and appreciate the poetic beauty of daily life in the New World. "Yet America is a poem in our eyes; its ample geography dazzles the imagination, and it will not wait long for metres."[21] The nation and its poets would have to grow up together, but the national material was now available for the kind of national writer that Mickiewicz and his Romantic allies were celebrating in Europe. If philosophy, literature, and poetry told the story of the people's truths, then every "people" could generate its own poets, stories, and truths. The nation was a poem that "dazzles the imagination." This national poem still had to be written, however, in the imaginative prophecy of poets and the imaginative memory of historians.

National Histories and National Identities

Memory shapes national identities in the way it shapes individual identities: It gives order and meaning to selected events and people in the past and provides narratives of continuity to establish a coherent identity in the present. Neither nations nor individuals can sustain identities if they have no memory of the past. Historians therefore contributed crucial literary service to modern nationalisms by describing the national meaning of the past and by showing connections between the living and dead. Yet nations (like individuals) protect their identities by forgetting or repressing the most painful conflicts of the past, and historians also helped people forget events that could challenge the dominant national story. As Ernest Renan (1823–1892) pointed out in a famous nineteenth-century essay, "the essence of a nation is that all individuals have many things in common, and also that they have forgotten many things."[22] The bitterness of past conflicts, the violence against unpopular persons, the brutal conquests of national territories, or the personal flaws of Founding Fathers tended to disappear from history. Or, more precisely, such events were transformed in popular national histories that celebrated the nation's unity, unique destiny, and virtuous early leaders. Forgetting was thus essential for the emergence of nationalisms because a *selective* memory protected national stories of unity and coherence.

The interplay of memory and forgetting produced the historical foundation for nationalist ideologies. Narratives about the national past gained coherence through the silence on certain contentious issues, but it was the coherence of a common history that supported the nationalist belief in a common cultural identity. "The nation," to continue with the themes of Renan's essay, ". . . is the culmination of a long past of endeavours, sacrifice, and devotion," which means that "a heroic past . . . is the social capital upon which one bases a national idea."[23] Although Renan was not a typical Romantic thinker, he clearly identified the cultural themes that brought Romanticism and nationalism together. Romanticism's emphasis on the specific rather than the universal traits of cultures, individuals, and historical eras became a central theme in both the amateur and professional histories that flooded the European literary market during the early nineteenth century.

Romantic assumptions helped shape new theories of history (often called historicism) that emphasized the unique characteristics of each historical era and culture.[24] Historians thus staked out their own claims for essential national work as they brought the nation's past culture into the consciousness of subsequent generations. Each age of history had its own spirit (*Zeitgeist*), just as each group of people had its own distinctive spirit (*Volksgeist*), but historians were needed to show how the spirit of a people expressed itself in particular events that may have been misinterpreted or forgotten. Romantic history, like Romantic poetry and philosophy, celebrated the creative expression and will of individual nations, whose character could appear in the personal actions of famous leaders or in the collective actions of entire populations. In either case, however, the nation could hear itself in the voice of the dead, and nationalists could appeal for new sacrifices to honor the memory of long-deceased ancestors.

Such themes appeared implicitly or explicitly in the national histories of all modern nations, but the most influential new theories of history emerged in Germany. Stressing the historical importance of languages and cultural differences, writers such as Herder and Fichte developed the philosophical underpinnings to support the study of distinctive national histories and to justify new actions in the name of old ideals. Fichte confidently assured his audiences that his call for national regeneration simply expressed the will of those Germans who could not speak from their graves. "Your forefathers unite themselves with these addresses," Fichte explained in one of his lectures, "and make a solemn appeal to you. Think that in my voice there are mingled the voices of your ancestors of the hoary past, who with their own bodies stemmed the onrush of Roman world-dominion, who with their blood won the independence of those mountains, plains, and rivers which under you have fallen a prey to the foreigner."[25] References to past sacrifices became a familiar theme of modern national histories, in part because such references carried a strong political message. If ancestors had sacrificed their blood and bodies to save the nation (the images were often religious), the present generation should not hesitate to make new sacrifices for those who would come later.

The emergence of professional historiography in the early nineteenth century pushed many historians away from Fichte's philosophical passion and rhetoric, but his assumptions about national differences reappeared in the most rigorous new historical studies—including the work of Leopold von Ranke (1795–1886). Although Ranke insisted that historians should build their arguments on documents and though he often advocated comparative or universal perspectives, he also placed the nation at the center of historical studies. National states were for Ranke the vital force in national histories, so his own studies typically dealt with the politics, diplomacy, and religious institutions of national elites. He shared the historicist belief in the uniqueness of each historical era and culture ("History leads us to unspeakable sweetness and refreshment at every place"), but he assumed that the specific spirit of each era emerged most clearly in the state. "It is obvious," he explained, "that each state has a completely definite character and a life of its own, which distinguishes it from all others."[26]

Historians thus gained access to the historical meaning of each era through the leaders and official policies of the state. Describing the "new development of the national spirit" in eighteenth-century Germany, for example, Ranke emphasized the distinctive accomplishments of the evolving Prussian state. He acknowledged that a "true politics can be sustained only by a great national existence," yet he attributed Germany's growing intellectual independence in the eighteenth century to a strong national leader, King Frederick II of Prussia. The culture needed a king:

> For a nation must feel itself independent in order to develop
> freely; and no literature ever flourished save when a great
> moment of history prepared the way. But it was strange that
> Frederick himself knew nothing of this, and hardly ex-
> pected it. He worked for the emancipation of the nation,
> and German literature worked with him, though he did not
> recognize his allies. But they knew him well. It made the
> Germans proud and bold to have had a hero arise from
> their midst.[27]

Such arguments in Ranke's work helped professionalize the historical account of national identities. This account of Frederick II, for example, noted the distinctiveness and independence of the German nation, suggested the links between cultures and states, pointed to national allegiances that were not altogether apparent to the past actors themselves, and traced a new sense of national pride and accomplishment to the influence of a great national leader. Ranke's approach to history thus reinforced the idea that nations were the active force in history, even as he rejected Fichte's philosophical rhetoric and wrote about state leaders instead of the language and soul of the people.

In contrast to Ranke's emphasis on national states, however, other national historians stayed closer to the linguists, poets, and philosophers who found the nation's spirit in the "people." This non-Rankean view of national histories flourished among a wide range of national historians (especially when they described nations that lacked states), yet one of the most influential historians of the "people" lived in the long-established French state. Jules Michelet (1798–1874) told the story of the French nation in a popular series of books that located the essential meaning of French history in the character of the French people. Although these people had revealed their strength and purpose in numerous events and historical eras, Michelet believed the French Revolution represented the purest expression of the deep, enduring national identity. He therefore celebrated the Revolution as the climactic moment of French history and as the nation's most generous contribution to modern world history. "The Revolution lives in ourselves,—in our souls," he explained at the beginning of a long book about its meaning and legacy, which he attributed to the grandeur of the "people" rather than to the famous revolutionary leaders.

> Great, astonishing results! But how much greater was the heart which conceived them! The deeds themselves are as nothing in comparison. So astonishing, indeed, was that greatness of heart, that the future may draw upon it for ever, without fearing to exhaust its resources. No one can approach its contemplation, without retiring a better man. Every soul dejected, or crushed with grief, every human or national heart has but to look there in order to find comfort: it is a mirror wherein humanity, in beholding itself, becomes once more heroic, magnanimous, disinterested.[28]

The disinterested sacrifice of that heroic French generation took many forms in Michelet's narrative, but it was the apparent unity of the French nation that elicited Michelet's strongest praise and nostalgia. Unlike those many historians who emphasized the Revolution's violent social and political conflicts, Michelet described a revolutionary era of harmony and shared purpose. "In the villages, especially, there are no longer either rich or poor, nobles or plebians; there is but one general table, and provisions are in common; social dissensions and quarrels have disappeared; enemies become reconciled."[29] Michelet's French Revolution became an imagined utopian community that somehow overcame the usual divisions of history and momentarily constructed a society in which national similarities overwhelmed every significant internal difference. Writing the story of the nation with the rhetorical skills of a brilliant narrative historian, he remembered the French Revolution by forgetting the bitter conflicts that challenged his account of national unity and purpose.

The French "people" thus became a remarkably coherent entity in Michelet's influential books. He saw himself as the spokesman for those people (dead and alive) who embodied the exceptional virtues of the French nation, though they had never been able to describe themselves in the language Michelet provided. He believed that he was in fact able "to establish the personality of the people" and to describe national qualities "which they have but do not understand."[30] Such writing obviously required historians who could bring the soul of the people into books, as Michelet assumed he had done in a popular book entitled simply *The People* (1846). Describing his approach to history in the preface to that book, Michelet explained that his writing went beyond a narrative or analysis to produce a *"resurrection;"* he brought the dead back to life. In an era when France's revolutionary achievements had been forgotten or denied, Michelet claimed to speak the national truths and traditions that were no longer heard. "I shall ever thank God for having given me this great France for my native land . . . ," he wrote in a typical statement of his national faith, "because I see her both as the representative of the liberties of all the world and as the country that links all the others together by sympathetic ties, the true introduction to universal love." As this passage suggests, Michelet invoked religious imagery to describe the remarkable sacrifices of the French nation and its gift to humanity. The history of France became for him the story of a messiah nation that had suffered and sacrificed its own life for the salvation of others, though the French people often failed to remember how that sacrifice had set them free. "So do not come and tell me how pale France is," Michelet wrote. "She has shed her blood for you." But this sacrifice was not just a gift to subsequent generations in France; it was also a sacrifice that offered life and freedom to the whole world, much as the death of Christ had offered hope for universal salvation. France "had to die and descend into the tomb in order that her living spirit might spread throughout the world. . . . The sword they plunged into her heart works miracles and heals. She converts her persecutors and teaches her enemies."[31]

The images of a sacrificed messiah nation may seem strange in the works of a prominent historian at the Collège de France, but such images indicate how historians resurrected the past to serve their vision of a revitalized national future. (Mickiewicz used similar metaphors at the Collège de France, where he regularly referred to Poland as the "Christ" of nations.) Michelet's rhetorical style gradually disappeared from professional historical writing, yet the claims for a distinctive national history, the references to exceptional national sacrifices, and the belief in unique national accomplishments would remain in all kinds of history books—including the textbooks that carried the national story into the schools of every modern state. These histories helped people place themselves in modern national cultures and also merged the story of the nation with familiar ancient narratives of religion and sacrifice. Michelet's history of France, like Fichte's history of Germany, repeated the oldest stories of life and death and resurrection, though the salvation in these new historical stories came from the nation instead of God.

Writing, Identity, and Difference

Modern nationalisms emerged out of political theories, political conflicts, and political revolutions that cannot be separated from the cultural history of writing. Political arguments for national sovereignty and national independence gained adherents and historical influence as they became integrated into the much wider history of writing and language in newspapers, novels, maps, poetry, philology, philosophy, and history. Nations were written and read into existence in places where governments already claimed to represent national populations and in other places where nationalists hoped to create new national states. In most cases national identities developed in conjunction with wars, military occupations, revolutions, or economic rivalries, but in every case the survival and diffusion of nationalism required the literary work of journalists, poets, philosophers, historians, and literary critics.

The construction of nations in writing often fused with the construction of nations in military or political conflicts, because the meaning of nations usually depended on narratives about cultural difference. According to nationalist writers, different languages, literatures, philosophies, histories, and social institutions created different nations and the rationale for different nation-states. Such differences could be obscure and complex, however, and they had to be explained to people who would not easily recognize the political significance of Latin and Germanic languages or the national meaning of past events and dead ancestors. Nationalism thus justified and shaped the intellectual labor of national writers and teachers, whose work in turn justified and shaped the nationalism of newspapers, schools, and history books. Most persons in these emerging national cultures did not understand or even hear about the complex nuances of national philosophers, poets, and historians, in part because they often did not yet know the national literary language.

The new writing nevertheless conveyed messages and produced policies that gradually extended the nation far beyond the educated elites. This cultural message overlapped with the political themes of nationalist movements and governments, generating modern ideological claims that even the most isolated persons would eventually encounter: The nation's unique political, cultural, and literary traditions or institutions separate it from other nations and call for sacrifices from each generation—occasionally in blood and almost always in education, labor, politics, and taxes. Modern people still faced the ancient problems of cooperation, conflict, survival, and death, but the meaning and organization of daily life became steadily more connected to the meaning and history of modern nations. Indeed for some persons in almost every modern society (including prominent writers such as Fichte, Mickiewicz, Michelet, and Mazzini), the nation offered a salvation that was anticipated or defended with all the fervor and poetry and ritual of an ancient religion.

4

Nationalism and Religion

Nationalism emerged in the overlapping spheres and interactions of politics, revolutions, state-building, language, literature, historical writing, and education, but even the combined force of all these political and cultural realities cannot adequately account for the intense emotional identifications that link individuals to modern nations. More people have died for their nations in modern times than for any other creed or political ideal—a remarkable historical pattern that raises some of the most complex questions about the meaning of nationalist ideas and identities. What ideals, commitments, and emotions enable people to view their own likely death or the deaths of their children as necessary and acceptable sacrifices to the collective interests of a nation? Why have so many people been willing to kill others in the name of their national governments or in pursuit of abstract national ideals?

Many persons have of course been compelled to serve in modern national armies, so the "power of nation-states" could provide one answer to my questions. Yet the coercive force of state power and propaganda does not really explain how modern nations have successfully mobilized public opinion in support of national wars and other dangerous or disruptive enterprises. Warfare may provoke the strongest popular support for national governments (at least when wars begin), but many nationalists make comparable sacrifices before they have a nation-state. More generally, modern people often respond with strong emotions when they encounter national symbols (flags, national monuments, military memorials) in everyday life. Defacement of a national flag, for example, regularly produces intense anger among those who see their national symbol attacked. Official condemnations of flag defacements do not in themselves generate such strong feelings of moral revulsion. Indeed, the moral passion that such defacements evoke suggests that the modern identification with national symbols often expresses the deep reverence and anxiety that people have long expressed for their highest religious ideals and their gods. It is precisely this emotion-laden commitment to "God and Country" that expresses the complex interaction of nationalism and religion in virtually every modern national culture.

One common account of the links between nationalism and religion emphasizes the importance of religions in defining the essential traits of a national identity. Irish nationalists, for example, might point to Catholicism as a crucial characteristic of the Irish nation, Israeli nationalists would insist on their nation's Judaism, some American nationalists have always claimed that Protestantism is the true creed of the United States, and many Iranians believe in the essential Islamic identity of their national state. Such connections between specific religions and national identities need to be examined in the historical analysis of particular nationalist ideologies, but the discussion of nationalism and religion here will stress the more general structural similarities of these two forms of thought. Instead of examining the Catholicism of Spain or the Protestantism of England, this chapter will note some of the ways in which nationalisms repeated, transformed, and fused with traditional Jewish and Christian ideas during the Age of Revolutions (1775–1850). To put the argument simply, much of the passionate commitment to nationalism and the willingness to die or kill for the nation emerged in the fusion of national and religious narratives about life and death.

Although the connections between nationalism and religion have attracted attention in many scholarly disciplines, the historian Carlton J. H. Hayes was one of the first to propose a comprehensive argument that continues to generate contemporary research. Writing shortly after the horrifying violence of World War I and responding to a wave of American religious fundamentalism in the 1920s, Hayes argued in an influential essay ("Nationalism as a Religion") that modern nations and nationalisms provide an integrating social and philosophical coherence that resembles the role of the Catholic Church in medieval Europe. From the day of their birth to the day of their death, modern people are registered, organized, mobilized, and consoled by the modern nation-state and the modern ideology of nationalism. Hayes himself accounted for nationalism's power by referring to a "religious sense" in the human psyche. During all eras of human history, Hayes argued, this "religious sense" in "man" has been expressed through "a mysterious faith in some power outside of himself, a faith always accompanied by feelings of reverence and usually attended by external acts and ceremonial." To be sure, many modern people have lost their faith in specific religious ideas, yet Hayes argued that even the skeptics typically "seek some object outside of themselves to which they might pay reverence." This search for a power outside and greater than the self, as Hayes described it, became a crucial source of nationalism's ideals and popularity. The nation offered connections to a transcendent reality and a system of beliefs to replace the faith in God that eighteenth-century skeptics had so famously questioned and rejected.[1]

Contemporary analysts have generally moved away from Hayes's emphasis on an essential human trait that can explain the historical power of nationalism. Stressing the interplay of religion and nationalism, recent accounts suggest that nationalism tended to merge with religion rather than to replace it.[2] Hayes nevertheless posed questions about the similarities and the emotional power of religion and nationalism that even the most antiessentialist historian must still confront. Despite the changing perspectives of historical research, we can still draw on Hayes's theory of cultural displacement (most notably, the transformation of Christianity into nationalism) to examine the influential religious themes in early nineteenth-century nationalist theories. Placed in the context of religious traditions, nationalism can be compared to other beliefs that offer consolations and explanations for violence, sacrifice, and power. The intersection of religion and the nation thus carries the analysis of nationalism from politics and writing into the psychology and history of human anxieties about death.

Nation as Salvation

Modern nationalisms first emerged in Western societies in which monotheism and Christian ethical ideals had shaped the dominant religious traditions. In this ancient Judeo-Christian conception of the links between divinity and human beings, individuals derived their purpose and meaning from their personal relation to a God who had existed before they were born and who would exist forever after they died. This transcendent Being entered into every phase and sphere of life, giving support and protection but also demanding commitments, loyalty, respect, and service. God thus gave each person a profound connection to eternal realities and to other people. As the theologians, priests, and pastors had explained since late antiquity, God understood the pains of human life, brought coherence and unity to human history, and offered the salvation of eternal life after human deaths.

The modern nation was not eternal, but it could rival religion in its comforting assurance of personal connections to a greater power that existed long before and after the life of every individual person. It could also resemble God insofar as it became the ultimate source of meaning and protection and as it provided the ties that bind otherwise isolated individuals into a shared (or imagined) community. Of course, the nation could also resemble God by demanding loyalty and service, but this demand was a familiar price that most people would pay for the benefits of protection, association, and identity. Although historians have repeatedly noted the similarities in these Christian and nationalist themes, the fusion of religion and nationalism was already recognized among the early-nineteenth-century theorists who sought to establish the highest possible authority for their nationalist arguments.

This often-claimed link with religious truths gave nationalists an ontological proof for the existence of the nations they admired. Michelet's account of the national soul in *The People*, for example, stressed a deep connection between individual persons and the creative power of their nation. "The Fatherland," Michelet argued, ". . . is for that soul of the people which dwells there the single and all-powerful means of realizing its nature, because it supplies both a vital point of departure and freedom to develop." The nation therefore became the vehicle for God's divine vision of human creativity and cooperation, which Michelet (like most Romantic nationalists) believed that modern nations could achieve on earth by cultivating their distinctive cultures *and* living in harmony with other nations.

> The more man advances [Michelet continued], the more he enters into the spirit of his country and the better he contributes to the harmony of the globe; he learns to recognize

his country . . . as a note in the grand concert; through it he himself participates and loves the world. The fatherland is the necessary initiation to the fatherland of all mankind.[3]

Metaphors of the father were thus transferred from God to the Nation as Michelet described the personal spiritual development that led the individual to a higher world beyond the self; and the Fatherland offered modern access to the ancient religious ideal of human cooperation.

The nation provided more than transcendence and human bonds, however, because it did not simply replace God in the worldview of most Romantic nationalists. In fact, duty to the nation was often described as something like a duty to God: Serving the nation offered new opportunities for honoring and serving God. Nobody promoted this fusion of God and country more fervently than the famous Italian writer Joseph Mazzini. In contrast to Michelet, Mazzini lived (like many Romantic nationalists) outside the national culture that he sought to represent and unify. His strongest national weapon was therefore a pen rather than a sword, but he had no doubt that he was wielding his weapon on behalf of a sacred cause. The Italian nation was for Mazzini an almost eternal being whose origins were older than ancient Rome and whose future lay beyond the vision of the most imaginative modern writers. Yet this extraordinary nation also required committed action from its people, as he explained constantly in writings that exhorted his compatriots to follow God's plan for their national destiny.

> The cry which rang out in all the great revolutions—the cry of the Crusades, *God wills it! God wills it!*—alone can rouse the inert to action, give courage to the fearful, enthusiasm of self-sacrifice to the calculating, faith to those who reject with distrust all merely human ideas. Prove to men that the work of emancipation and of progressive development to which you call them is part of God's design. . . .
>
> God wills it—God wills it! It is the cry of the People, O Brothers! it is the cry of *your* People, the cry of the Italian Nation.[4]

Mazzini thus invoked divine will as the most compelling justification for his imagined society of Italian unity and republicanism, thereby translating the oldest religious duty (serve God) into the national political campaigns and conflicts of nineteenth-century Europe.

Although Mazzini accepted the Romantic assumption that different nationalities could cooperate in a "harmonious concert" of nations, he also assumed that God had given Italy an exceptionally important responsibility in world history. This belief in unique national destinies became another typical religious theme among nationalists who described their own national populations as the "Chosen People" of history. This particular strand of nationalist thought drew especially on the ancient Hebrew belief in God's unique concern for the people of Israel, but it first became a central theme in the modern nationalisms of Protestant societies.

The emergence of early national feeling in Britain owed a great deal to the Protestant opposition to Catholicism and Catholic Spain during the sixteenth century, and the Protestant influence on early American national identity may have been even more pronounced.[5] Puritan religious accounts of a new "City on the Hill," for example, helped generate a narrative of the Chosen People that would contribute decisively to the American Revolution and the subsequent development of America's national ideology. European Protestants had meanwhile established national churches that depended on and enhanced the power of national governments. Church-state alliances provided strong institutional support for the fusion of religion and nationalism in northern European nations such as England and Germany. The popular religious traditions of pietism merged with a new national movement to produce typical descriptions of German society as a privileged center of God's plan for the world. "I can never despair of my fatherland," wrote Friedrich Schliermacher (1768–1834) in a letter (1809) that expressed views that were also common in English and American writings about *their* nations. "I believe too firmly in it, I know too definitely that it is an instrument and a people chosen by God."[6]

The religious images of a Chosen People offered another opportunity to define the differences that gave each national culture its own identity. Although these religious definitions of difference became especially important in many Protestant nationalisms, they also contributed to new nationalisms in predominantly Catholic countries such as Italy and Poland. Adam Mickiewicz's Polish nationalism, for example, rested on a whole series of Messianic claims about the unique spiritual achievements and sufferings of the Polish people, all of which separated their Slavic identity from other people and promised future achievements for a united Polish nation. In contrast to modern secular nations, Mickiewicz explained from exile in Paris, Slavs had "the humility, the gentleness, [and] the patience that characterized the martyrs of the early medieval church." Such traits gave the Slavic religion an unparalleled "purity" that might well show modern people the way to a new, higher morality. "The Slavs alone have the advantage of having conserved the early [Christian] tradition in all the purity [and] natural sentiment of the divinity," Mickiewicz argued in a narrative about the overlapping histories of religion, literature, and nationality. This legacy of pure religion sustained an identity that later Slavs were obliged to honor through their defense of a distinctive national culture, but Mickiewicz believed they possessed both the will and the knowledge to uphold their religious traditions. In contrast to other nations, the Slavs had never abandoned their religious beliefs for the false gods of science or literature or philosophy. "They therefore truly form a separate race."[7]

Religious history thus gave Mickiewicz and other nationalists a narrative to explain the unique sufferings of specific nations (all Chosen People had to undergo special tribulations), but the millennial perspectives in the Christian tradition could also be used to portray past or present crises as the prelude to a happier future. The Chosen People always had good spiritual reasons to expect a coming millennium of peace, prosperity, justice, and freedom.

The nationalists' belief in the special mission of their own nations gave universal significance to what might otherwise appear to be the local problems of a small population or specific culture. Situated in a religious narrative of suffering and redemption, the endless struggle for national independence and unity became an essential contribution to human progress and the development of world history. Each generation faced the tasks of identifying the national mission and promoting this mission in a wider world of politics, culture, and work. The national mission might well seem daunting to the would-be nationalist, but it was precisely the grandeur of the mission that accounted for the sacrifices and suffering on its behalf. Here again the ancient religious language (witness for your faith in the world) offered a model for nationalists who translated the religious injunction into a new call for service to the nation. Mazzini's commentary on Italian duties to the nation, for example, included repeated assurances that Italy's mission carried hope and implications for the entire modern world. "Our country is our field of labor," he wrote; "the products of our activity must go forth from it for the benefit of the whole earth. . . . In labouring according to true principles for our country we are labouring for Humanity. . . . Your Country is the token of the mission which God has given you to fulfil in humanity."[8]

But what was this unique Italian mission and what did it require? Mazzini informed his readers that Italy was to provide "the moral unity of Europe." This task obviously imposed "immense duties" on all Italians, yet it was a mission for which Italians were uniquely prepared. A long history of unifying achievements in ancient Rome and early medieval Christianity had shown that the Italians knew how to bring moral unity to all the people of Europe—though this unique Italian mission also called for the strictest moral virtue. "Your duties to your Country are proportioned to the loftiness of this mission. You have to keep it pure from egoism, [and] uncontaminated by falsehood."[9] The new servants of the nation were for Mazzini the successors of the ancient missionaries of the church, and their new national mission required the devotion, self-sacrifice, and piety of the early Christians.

Such rhetoric offered little more than asceticism and a futile idealism for modern, skeptical readers, but the reward for Mazzini or Mickiewicz (and their many sympathetic followers) would come in the exalted status of the nation. If devotion to God could bring salvation for the loyal believer, then surely devotion to God's country could ensure a similar salvation for the new nationalist. In fact, nationalists such as Michelet and Mickiewicz regularly compared the suffering of a nation and its believers to the sufferings of Christ and his believers. The consolations in both cases came in the expectation of ultimate redemption for all who shared in the pain. The story of the nation thus became the story of Christ, as Mickiewicz explicitly claimed in his famous account of Messianic Poland (1832):

> On the third day the soul shall return to the body, and the Nation shall arise and free all the peoples of Europe from slavery.
> And already two days have gone by. One day ended with the first capture of Warsaw, and the second day ended with the second capture of Warsaw, and the third day shall begin, but shall not end.
> And as after the resurrection of Christ blood sacrifices ceased in all the world, so after the resurrection of the Polish nation wars shall cease in all Christendom.[10]

Mickiewicz carried the narrative of the Chosen People, national mission, and national salvation farther into the realm of religious speculation than many of his contemporaries, but the themes of his messianic nationalism also appeared in more muted forms throughout the writings of most early-nineteenth-century nationalists.

Claims for the universal significance of national events or movements could be found in nationalisms from America to Russia as national writers translated religious conceptions of transcendence, unity, duty, and mission into stories of national purpose and destiny. Successful nationalisms frequently merged with and sometimes replaced many of the oldest religious aspirations in Western cultures, including the desire to emulate Christ and the desire to find life after death. At the same time, however, the replication or translation of ancient religious traditions went beyond nationalist theologies into the equally important symbols and rituals of new nations and nationalisms.

The Symbols and Rituals of Religions and Nations

The images and metaphors that nationalists used to describe their nations in the early nineteenth century overlapped with the familiar icons and languages of Christian churches. As Mazzini noted in one of his typical summaries of the new faith, "Your country should be your Temple. God at the summit, a People of equals at the base."[11] This image ignored the possibility of conflicts between the nation and God; indeed, it suggested a remarkable continuity in these two transcendent entities, both of which could be honored in the service to a truly national state. Although some theologians still debated ancient questions about human duties to "Caesar and Christ," most nationalists assumed that the fusion of national and religious ideals confirmed the ultimate authority and wisdom in both forms of truth. "Heaven and earth must unite themselves in Germany," a patriotic German pastor explained to his parishioners during the Napoleonic wars. "The church must become a state in order to gain power and the state must become a church in order to be the kingdom of God."[12] Given such assumptions among the clergy, it was easy enough for nationalists in Germany and other modern cultures to extend the emotional meaning of religious beliefs into a deep reverence for the new symbols of a nation.

As Carlton Hayes and other analysts have noted, there were nationalist analogues for almost every traditional religious symbol, book, ritual, saint, holiday, and moral lesson.[13] The national flag of each national movement, for example, became a powerful, sacred symbol, evoking the kind of respect that had long been directed toward the symbolic Christian cross or the religious relics in famous churches. Elaborate rituals were developed to honor national flags, and desecration of flags became a new form of sacrilege or blasphemy. Most national movements represented themselves with a flag before they had established an independent state, which meant that flags offered symbolic alternatives to reigning regimes as well as

French-Polish Committee National Flags. Illustration for the committee by an unknown artist, 1831. Marquis de Lafayette Print Collection, David Bishop Skillman Library, Lafayette College.

National flags evoke shared identities and symbolic unities. The flags of France and Poland were linked in this image to illustrate a unified, international movement that sought (unsuccessfully) to secure Polish independence from Russia in the early 1830s. Note the references to liberty and the images of the French cock and the Polish eagle, which symbolized national freedom with familiar allusions to nature.

the power of well-established nation-states. The famous red, white, and blue tricolor flag in France, for example, symbolized a liberal opposition to the conservative Bourbon government that restored both the monarchy and the traditional royal flag after the fall of Napoleon (1814–1830). German nationalists were also using an illegal black, red, and gold tricolor flag during these same years to express their opposition to the Austrian Prince Metternich and to symbolize their political and cultural aspirations for a new unified German state. Other nationalisms turned to the natural world for symbols such as the eagle to represent the autonomy or independence of distinctive national cultures.

In addition to their flags and other symbolic icons, nationalists regularly praised national documents or literary works with the reverence that religious leaders brought to their study of the Bible and other ancient religious texts. Every nationalism and nation identified essential sources of national unity and truth in a canon of written texts, which could include declarations of national independence and rights, national constitutions, great works of national literature, the words of national anthems, and even the famous speeches of national orators. Students read the sanctified national texts at school, and nationalist leaders invoked their authority to explain or justify all kinds of public action. The American Declaration of Independence and national Constitution, for example, quickly became sacred texts in the United States, where the typical nineteenth-century Independence Day rituals celebrated the wisdom and virtue of both the documents and their authors. Political documents were also important in European nationalisms, but literature was often a more valuable resource for defining national unity. Despite the divisive political conflicts within each nation or national movement, the English could celebrate Shakespeare as their national literary treasure, the French could praise Molière, Racine, or Voltaire, the Italians could honor Dante, and the Germans could remember Luther. The famous political and literary texts of various national cultures thus came to resemble canonical religious works insofar as they defined a national creed and provided a shared cultural resource for citations, reinterpretations, and praise. Nobody could denounce the sacred texts of his or her own nation and retain political or cultural influence in the nationalist movement. The sacred national texts often attracted even more respect than the older religious texts because people who disagreed about religion could still agree on the wisdom of a national constitution or the genius of Shakespeare. Religious education thus evolved into national education, and the recitation of religious catechisms gave way to the recitation of national poets or the last words of national martyrs.

The sanctified texts of the nation often fused with images of sacred national figures, who symbolically embodied the highest national ideals. Like the stories of saints and virtuous actions in the religious tradition, the story of George Washington or Joan of Arc or Martin Luther showed how the virtuous figures in a national culture served the national cause with unbending commitment, integrity, and self-sacrifice. Founding Fathers and other exemplary national leaders therefore represented or interpreted the meaning of the nation much as Moses, Jesus, and Mohammed had interpreted the meaning of God. The status of such national leaders in the civil religions of nationalism could in fact be compared to the status of the great founding figures in the ancient religious traditions.

National heroes might have expressed the national spirit in the realm of politics, warfare, religion, or literature, but their achievements in every case offered inspiration for nationalists who might despair about the status or survival of the nation in their own time. Fichte's account of Martin Luther, for example, suggested that this national hero had confronted and overcome sixteenth-century dangers that were every bit as threatening as the dangers facing Germans in the Napoleonic era. "That this man . . . fearlessly and in all earnestness went to meet all the devils in hell," Fichte wrote, "is natural and in no way a wonder. Here we have a proof of German earnestness of soul." But how did Luther embody the qualities of a whole nation? According to Fichte, the Germans "renounced all, endured all tortures, and fought in bloody and indecisive wars" in order to maintain their independence and their reformed religion; neither Luther nor the German people would surrender their religious principles to foreign leaders or outside forces. Luther was therefore the highest expression of a distinctive national soul ("Behold in this a proof of the characteristic quality of the German people") and a model for latter-day struggles against those who welcomed or accepted the French occupation of Berlin.[14]

The history of national heroes in the writings of Fichte and other nationalist authors always stood in stark contrast to the history of skeptics or traitors who had lost their national faith. In fact, nationalists typically identified evil figures whose corruption or betrayal of the nation would be familiar to anyone who knew the Biblical story of Judas Iscariot. National traitors were the modern heretics: persons who went astray, deceived others, and deserved the most severe punishments. These national heretics could be famous people (e.g., General Benedict Arnold in America) or part of a secret conspiracy (e.g., émigrés and spies in revolutionary France), but their role in national narratives resembled the role of Satan in religious narratives. Nationalists were therefore eager to expose and revile all presumed national traitors and heretics, especially since such traitors could be expected to operate with satanic deception. Unmasking the most conspicuous national heretics was not enough to ensure the national survival, however, because there were other, more widespread dangers in the general indifference toward national ideals and national objectives. Like the prophets of ancient Israel or the pastors in Protestant pulpits, nationalists often warned that their own generation lacked the national faith and commitments of earlier generations.

The national story could thus become a religious story of dangerous moral decline in which people betrayed the national cause to pursue their own selfish gains or to adopt the ideas and customs of other nations. To be sure, nationalists anticipated a better future for their nations like religious leaders anticipated a better world to come, but the road to that better world was filled with temptations to abandon or ignore the higher cause. In short, people could forget about the nation as readily as they could forget about God. Anxious jeremiads therefore appeared in nationalist literatures and warned weak nationalists with the admonitions of a church sermon. When Mazzini condemned those who would no longer defend the national cause, for example, he urged his allies to "thrust them from your ranks; for whoso is not ready to testify to his faith with his blood is no believer." The temptations of lethargy and despair could always overwhelm the faith in a better future, but Mazzini insisted that the "cross of misfortune and persecution" was simply the prelude to a new age of harmony and cooperation. "Let your lips not utter the cry of hate, nor the conspirator's hollow phrase," he explained in an essay ("Faith and the Future") for those who might have lost faith in the cause, "but the tranquil, solemn word of the days that are to come."[15] Mazzini's good nationalists therefore needed vigilance and perseverance to withstand the dangers of decline and betrayal, but the steadfast believers would arrive finally in a better, more harmonious future.

The sacred figures, texts, and prophets of nationalisms were remembered and honored in public places that became the national equivalents of the sanctified spaces in which religious believers had always expressed their devotion and commitment to God. Advocates of national creeds sanctified the birthplaces or tombs of national heroes, the sites of famous battles, and cemeteries of unknown soldiers. Every nation-state created monuments and memorials to celebrate the achievements and sacrifices of national armies or great generals (for example, the Arc de Triomphe in France, Trafalgar Square in Britain, Arlington National Cemetery in the United States).[16] The greatest monuments were usually erected in capital cities, but even small villages would eventually construct memorials to deceased soldiers and heroes. Such monuments attracted visitors and symbolized national identities in the same way that famous cathedrals had symbolized the ideals and identities of medieval towns. Visits to places such as Napoleon's tomb (constructed in 1840)

Procession of Napoleon's Funereal Cortege. Lithograph by Victor Adam, c. 1840. From the copy in the Rare Book Collection, The University of North Carolina, Chapel Hill.

National monuments created new sites for popular national pilgrimages. The return of Napoleon's body for burial in Paris, for example, offered an occasion for nationalist rituals in 1840. Napoleon's tomb became a new national shrine and a new attraction for visitors to the French capital. The inscription below this lithograph reports that "It was truly a triumphal procession worthy of the great People who attended . . . and of the hero who was honored."

or George Washington's home at Mount Vernon appeared on the itineraries of modern tourists, whose pilgrimages to national monuments became as common as medieval pilgrimages to sacred shrines. National monuments conveyed the lessons of national histories and sacrifices in images that could be compared to the representations of Christian history and sacrifices in great churches. Indeed, the rituals and speeches at national monuments on national holidays often resembled the rituals of religious holidays in urging remembrance of deaths that had given life to the nation. Such rituals promoted the ideals of national unity and offered annual opportunities for nationalists to remind their compatriots about the duties and rewards of national identity.

The calls for national sacrifice did not simply replace older religious rituals, however, because the churches remained an important center for national messages and remembrances. Linking religious duty to national duty, the clergy often helped the nationalist cause by adding theological justifications for national commitments and sacrifices, especially during times of warfare. Religious leaders in late-eighteenth-century America, for example, regularly interpreted the American revolutionary war as a divinely inspired event in which good patriots could serve God by joining the struggle against Britain. A Protestant pastor named Abraham Keteltas assured his congregation in Massachusetts (1777) that the American cause was also "the cause of God." Noting the evils and oppressions of the British government, Keteltas claimed that Americans were defending and promoting the divine plan for justice and freedom on earth. "It is the cause of heaven against hell," he explained. "It is the cause for which heroes have fought, patriots bled, prophets, apostles, martyrs, confessors, and righteous men have died. Nay, it is a cause for which the Son of God came down from his celestial throne and expired on the cross."[17]

This image of Christ's sacrifice for humanity provided the most compelling precedent and model for those many nationalists who merged the cause of God and nation in virtually every European and American culture. Comparisons between Christ and other human sacrifices for or by a nation gave a Messianic dimension to national ideologies that have never been called "Messianic nationalisms," though their advocates repeatedly invoked ancient religious conceptions of death and resurrection. Among all the overlapping symbols and rituals of religion and nationalism, the Christlike images of sacrifice and death for others provided the most powerful summary of what nations could ultimately require from their people. People who gave their lives to save the nation were thus the most hallowed figures in every nationalist ideology—and the story of the nation was always a story about life and death.

Death, Sacrifice, and Warfare

Nationalist accounts of the connection between individual lives and the nation often suggested that nations provided a consoling form of immortality. Although individuals inevitably had to die, they continued to live in a collective national memory that preserved their language, their ideas, and their institutions. Ancient human desires for a life after death could thus evolve from the realm of theology into the realm of nationalism, in which people could find strong moral inducements for risking their own lives or the lives of their children in long national wars. Breaking with older patterns of monarchical warfare that mostly promoted royal dynastic interests or the military careers of nobles, modern wars came to be seen as national crusades against infidels whose alien customs or beliefs threatened the existence of one's own nation. Death in battle against such enemies might not send the soul to heaven, but it would definitely earn eternal gratitude from a nation whose survival depended on the sacrifices of its soldiers.

The military force that could bring death to the nation's youth and the nation's enemies thus brought life to the nation as a whole. Images of immortality and resurrection abounded in early-nineteenth-century nationalist commentaries that celebrated the life-giving force of national communities. Ernst Moritz Arndt reported from Germany during the anti-Napoleonic wars (1813), for example, that a military parade gave him a sense of eternal life that he could find nowhere else. "I feel the indestructible life," he wrote in a description of the national army, "the eternal spirit, and the eternal God. . . . [In this moment] I am no longer a single suffering man, I am one with the Volk and God."[18] Arndt's desire to connect himself to an immortal national existence suggests the deep emotional anxiety (fear of death) that nationalism helped to assuage: people die, but nations can live forever.

Fichte developed a philosophical summary of this emotional desire for immortality in his *Addresses to the German Nation*. Individuals placed the survival of the nation above the mere physical survival of themselves, Fichte explained, because they knew that future generations would remember and honor their sacrifices for the national

Entry of the Emperor in Berlin. Engraving and aquatint by L. J. Allais and Cotteau, after a sketch by Debret, c. 1807. From the copy in the Rare Book Collection, The University of North Carolina, Chapel Hill.

The French occupation of Prussia—represented here in a French image of Prussian subservience as Napoleon enters Berlin—provoked a profound nationalist reaction among numerous German intellectuals. The military debacle pushed writers such as J. G. Fichte and E. M. Arndt to develop new philosophical definitions of German national identity.

cause. "The noble-minded man's belief in the eternal continuance of his influence even on this earth is thus founded on the hope of the eternal continuance of the people from which he has developed." Individual lives and deaths thus acquired meaning and purpose through this link to the nation, and death itself was an entirely acceptable price to pay for the continuing life of the nation.

> Hence, the noble-minded man will be active . . . and will sacrifice himself for his people. Life merely as such, the mere continuance of changing existence, has in any case never had any value for him; he has wished for it only as the source of what is permanent. But this permanence is promised to him only by the continuous and independent

existence of his nation. In order to save his nation he must
be ready even to die that it may live, and that he may live in
it the only life for which he has ever wished.[19]

Fichte's description of immortality, in other words, shows how traditional Christian conceptions of salvation entered into new beliefs
about the saving grace of nations. Human beings needed nations in
order to find the "permanence" that physical existence could never
provide, but this eternal source of meaning (like God) required service and sacrifice. Although serving the nation might well cause personal pain, it was the kind of virtuous action that ennobled human
beings and ensured a life after death.

Nationalist narratives about sacrifice thus merged with the nationalist interest in history, because the immortality of deceased patriots
depended on the memory of the nation. Given this moral duty to
remember the virtues of the dead, historians contributed to the nationalist ideology by urging later generations to emulate the
commitments and sacrifices of their ancestors. Fichte reminded his
audiences of courageous Germans who had "willingly poured out
their blood" for posterity, thereby saving the nation and giving
nineteenth-century Germans an example of what they must do for
their descendents.[20] The gift of blood and bodies was of course a familiar religious theme in every nationalist ideology, but the blood
was simply the prelude to a new national life or resurrection. "Fight
as Italians," Mazzini told his compatriots, "so that the blood which
you shed may win honour and love, not for you only, but for your
Country. And may the constant thought of your soul be for Italy."[21]

The images of blood and sacrifice and death suggest how the links
between nationalism and religion could transform warfare into the
highest expression of national identity. Wars revealed the dangers of
evil enemies and the coherent purpose of one's own nation more
clearly than any other historical event. No matter how much a nation's people might differ or disagree among themselves, their essential unity appeared forcefully in their opposition to foreign enemies.
The unity and survival of every nation therefore depended on people who were willing to fight the nation's enemies, even or especially
if they must sacrifice their own lives in the struggle. Soldiers became
the highest embodiment of the national ideal because they died to
give life and freedom to others.

Nationalism's link to warfare gave a strong military flavor to
many forms of nationalist culture, including historical writing, art,

flags, parades, monuments, uniforms, and national anthems. The words of national anthems, for example, frequently referred to the military struggles that defined or clarified the meaning of nations. Songs such as "The Star-Spangled Banner" in America (1814) and "The Marsaillaise" in France (1792) clearly indicated that nations ultimately survived with flags waving in the "rockets' red glare" and "bombs bursting in air." Rouget de Lisle described the French national mission in "The Marsaillaise" by emphasizing the dangers of an enemy that came "to cut the throats of your sons." In typical nationalist optimism, however, he insisted that the violence would lead to a final French victory. "Fight with your defenders," Rouget de Lisle implored, "under our flags, so that victory / Will rush to your manly strains; / That your dying enemies / Should see your triumph and glory!"[22] National wars thus offered a high road to national salvation. To be sure, the nation's military struggles could be as dangerous and difficult as the Christian's struggle against evil, yet both the patriot and the believer could see the battle as a necessary sacrifice for the better world to come.

Meanwhile, service to the nation was a "manly" task for soldiers who set out to defend their "mother country" or "Fatherland" with all the passion of a child defending a parent. Indeed, the nation would often be compared to a family, thus fusing conceptions of gender and sexuality with religious conceptions of duty, immortality, and sacrifice. Men could make the highest sacrifices to the nation in warfare, but women made their own extraordinary commitment by sacrificing their children to the national cause. For every Christlike soldier's death, there was a Madonna-like mother or wife. In short, the overlapping themes of nationalism, religion, and war fused also with social, cultural, and political definitions of men and women.

The Fusion of Nationalism and Religion

Some analysts of nationalism have argued that the faith in nations replaced ancient religious beliefs and became a new secular religion. This kind of replacement theory may accurately describe the ideology of a few fervent nationalists, but most modern nationalisms have managed to fuse religious and political ideals. Nationalists have often retained numerous religious assumptions, including a belief in God and clearly delineated ethical conceptions of good and evil. More generally, most nationalisms attracted adherents by expanding rather than replacing religious accounts of transcendence, unity, and sacrifice. Belief in a higher, metaphysical world had always given Europeans a way to understand their place in the material world, so the nation could take its place within this cultural tradition as a new mediating link between individuals and the higher realm of virtue and immortality.

In any case, it is significant that the first systematic narratives of nationalism appeared in Western societies, in which the ancient Biblical narratives (Hebrew and Christian alike) had long influenced philosophy, literature, political theory, historical writing, and social rituals. Almost all the ancient religious themes could be adapted to fit into stories about nations: descriptions of a Chosen People, beliefs in a distinctive moral mission, explanations of current sufferings as the prelude to a more harmonious future, and reverence for the life-giving sacrifice of blood and bodies. Such ideas circulated in modern national cultures through sanctified flags, texts, liturgies, holidays, monuments, and memorials to saintly national heroes, all of which also resembled the symbols and rituals of Judeo-Christian religious traditions. The identity-shaping power of national-religious ideas and symbols appeared most conspicuously in new national wars, when nationalist movements and nation-states used the language of religious crusades to explain and justify their violent conflicts with national enemies. In the French revolutionary wars against old regime Europe and the German wars against Napoleonic France, for example, nationalist leaders urged the nation to purify itself and make painful sacrifices. In return for this commitment, good patriots received assurances about the survival of the nation after their death; immortality would be found in a culture that could not die. Indeed, popular images of soldiers (who gave their lives for others) and their nation (which suffered for the greater good of humanity) drew meaning from ancient Christian images of Christ, so that the story of the Messiah often reappeared implicitly or explicitly in the stories of nations.

This fusion of nationalist and Biblical ideas could of course produce tensions and contradictions as well as an ideological merger—and there were always religious thinkers who questioned or rejected the "false gods" of nationalism. Roman Catholic conceptions of the universal church, for example, offered attractive theoretical alternatives to nationalist conceptions of competing, conflicting nations. Similarly, Christian injunctions to love one's enemies could be invoked in opposition to every national war. Yet the religious plea to respect and love enemies was typically ignored in the nationalist embrace of other ancient religious ideas that could be readily translated

Grenadier on Elba Island. Lithograph by Pinçon, after a painting by
Horace Vernet, c. 1840. From the copy in the Rare Book Collection, The
University of North Carolina, Chapel Hill.

Nationalisms typically celebrate the soldier as the ideal embodiment
of the nation's strength and virtues, in part because soldiers sacrifice
their lives to save their people from foreign dangers. This portrait of a
grenadier shows a strong, well-armed soldier who stands ready for the
next call to duty, which will soon come from a national commander on
the hill behind him.

into modern narratives of national destiny. Nationalists found valuable religious parallels to their own creeds in dichotomies that contrasted good against evil, eternal against temporary, and sacrifice against self-interest.

Political abstractions and the desire for national economic development simply could not generate the nationalist moral passion that made death an acceptable sacrifice for national causes. And even the most comprehensive study of national histories and literatures was unlikely to sustain a soldier in battle. For most people, therefore, the national cause could only evoke the requisite emotional attachments when it became linked to the oldest human anxieties about survival, death, and immortality. Religious accounts of God, moral order, and life after death had long provided the most important, consoling explanations for these inevitable limitations and pains of human life, and nationalism could destroy neither the anxieties nor the traditional responses to them.

Nationalist ideologies and rituals nevertheless offered new consolations for death and new justifications for moral crusades; nationalist moral dichotomies fused with religious moral dichotomies to define the transcendent meaning of national identities; and new definitions of national identity and difference drew on familiar religious definitions of cultural identity and difference to explain and deepen the emotional meaning of nationalism. At the same time, however, both nationalism and religion became deeply entangled with identity-shaping conceptions of gender and race, all of which added other emotions and psychological complexities to the quest for national unity and coherence.

5

Nationalism, Gender, and Race

Nationalism has always generated the strongest emotional power when nationalist ideas have overlapped with other components of individual and group identities. Although all national ideologies and identities evolve through the symbols and conflicts of human cultures, the individuals within a national culture often merge their national identities with other phenomena or traits that seem to be "natural" rather than historical. National identities can thus become associated with climate or geography, for example, and they have regularly been linked with the apparently natural realities of sexuality, gender, and race. Ideas about gender and race resemble ideas about nations in that a person's gender and racial traits are taken to be rooted in nature (like the primordial history of a national population). In this view, people are simply born as girls or boys, and as "black," "red," "yellow" or "white," much as they are born German or Chinese, French or American.

Recent historical studies generally challenge such essentialized conceptions of gender and race by stressing that the apparently "natural" traits of individuals and groups are in fact shaped more by culture than by biological inheritance.[1] People learn the meaning of their gender and race through the families, schools, religions, laws, and political systems that also teach them the meaning of their nationality. There are of course physical characteristics that differenti-ate the sexes, and people inherit different skin pigmentations, but these physical differences acquire their historical significance in the ideologies and hierarchies of social and cultural institutions. As these institutions became "nationalized" during the nineteenth century, the meaning of both gender and race became increasingly entwined with the ideologies of modern nationalism.

Nationalism flourished by connecting the intimate, personal spheres of individual lives with the public spheres of politics and collective identity. Such connections developed most powerfully in modern conceptions of the family, reproduction, and personal re-spectability, all of which suggested that a "good" citizen was also a responsible member of a family (and vice versa). Ideas and anxieties about the family also fused in many nationalisms with other ideas and anxieties about the biological meaning of race or racial purity, so that nationalist claims about distinctive histories, languages, reli-gions, and political institutions gradually merged in the nineteenth century with other claims about distinctive national families or racial traits. Descriptions of sexuality, gender, and race thus became linked to descriptions of national identity, especially when nationalists sought to define the (imagined) purity of a nation's culture or the prospects for a nation's future development.

The meaning of gender and race emerged like the meaning of na-tions through definitions of difference or "otherness," but the differ-ent genders and racial groups within nations meant that demarca-tions of difference defined *internal* social categories as well as the boundaries that separated national cultures from other nations. The existence of a nation required relations between women and men as surely as it required the memory and forgetting of history, and each generation had to learn the meaning of sexuality, gender, family, and race while it was also learning the meaning of national history.

Gender Identities, Families, and Nationalist Ideologies

Narratives about the imagined communities of modern nations rely constantly on metaphorical and political allusions to families and family relationships. Evoking the emotional charge of the most com-plex family attachments, nationalist writings are typically filled with affectionate references to the "fatherland," "mother tongue" and "mother country," "brothers-in-arms," "founding fathers," and the "national family." The revolutionary celebration of "fraternity," for example, emerged as the most important nationalist theme in a postrevolutionary French political culture that remained profoundly divided over the meaning of liberty and equality; and the new legal management of families in the Napoleonic Code became a more permanent component of French national life than all the military campaigns in the Napoleonic wars. The nation-state entered widely into all phases of family life (from births and marriages to deaths and inheritances), thus displacing the Church from domestic spheres that had long been the province of religion.

More generally, nationalist writers and political activists in the early nineteenth century defined national identities in terms of stereotypical gender traits that tended to emphasize the "manly" virtues of good nations in contrast to the deceptions and corruptions of bad nations. The British portrayed their wars against revolutionary and Napoleonic France in such gendered terms by describing themselves as the masculine opponents of an essentially effeminate French society. This image of Britain's "masculinity," as the historian Linda Colley notes, appeared in the self-defined British tendency to be "bluff, forthright, rational, [and] down-to-earth," whereas the feminine French were said to be "subtle, intellectually devious, preoccupied with high fashion, fine cuisine and etiquette, and . . . obsessed with sex."[2] Interpreted from this perspective, the military conflict between Britain and France could be linked to other strong feelings among British nationalists who saw the national struggle as a kind of war between the sexes in which positive (male) and negative (female) sexual characteristics shaped the combatants on both sides of the battlefield.

Most modern nations and nationalist movements developed male or female national symbols that were supposed to represent national strengths and virtues to both the citizens at home and foreigners. The meaning of England appeared in images of Britannia and John Bull, the Germans represented themselves with Germania, and the Americans eventually produced Uncle Sam. French revolutionaries embraced the famous allegorical figure of "Marianne," who symbolized national virtue for republican groups throughout France during the nineteenth century. This "personification of the Republic as a female allegory," notes the leading historian of Marianne's importance in French culture, became an "object of affection that sometimes reached quasi-religious proportions."[3] If the various national populations found it difficult to understand the abstract meanings of their national histories or political institutions, they could turn to the reassuring, gendered images of national identities that gradually re-

The Triumph of the French Republic under the Auspices of Liberty (detail).
Pen and ink with watercolor and gouache, by an anonymous artist, c.
1793. Ackland Art Museum, The University of North Carolina, Chapel
Hill, Ackland Fund.

The French Republic was regularly portrayed as a woman. She sits
here with her arm on the female figure of liberty, who wears the
Phrygian cap, and beneath the female figure of truth, who holds an
open book and sends forth a beam of light. The gendered allegories
suggested that defense of the nation resembled the male defense of
mothers, wives, or daughters (note the male Hercules), and loyalty to
the nation resembled loyalty to a family.

placed religious saints and monarchs in the symbolic representation
of national cultures.

This fusion of gender and national identities provided analytical
categories for all kinds of nineteenth-century writers, including social theorists, historians, and the authors of travel books. When the

French theorist Arthur de Gobineau (1816–1882) published his ideas on race and nationality, for example, he defined nations according to their gender as well as their race—arguing that "the male nations look principally for material well-being, the female nations were more taken up with the needs of the imagination."[4] Of course an ideal nation might well combine male and female attributes, as the American Ralph Waldo Emerson (writing at the same time as Gobineau) suggested in his account of the well-balanced English national identity. "They are rather manly than warlike," Emerson wrote. "When the war is over, the mask falls from the affectionate and domestic tastes, which make them women in kindness. . . . The two sexes are co-present in the English mind." Indeed, according to Emerson, the fundamental traits of English culture could be found in the gendered traditions that had merged to form English society: "Mixture is a secret of the English island; and, in their dialect, the male principle is the Saxon; the female, the Latin; and they are combined in every discourse."[5] Emerson generally admired English culture, and his gendered explanations pointed to historical achievements from which America's own dominant culture had evolved, but the wider cultural implication of his commentary emerged in his typical nineteenth-century inclination to connect national identity to the identities of women and men.

The overlapping, contrasting, and connected identities of women, men, and nations became a prominent theme in nationalist writings about families. Most nationalists were highly interested in ideas about the family, though they often used this word to describe the imagined family of a whole nation as well as the domestic family of specific parents, children, and households. These two concepts of family were inseparable for most nationalists, because they assumed that a strong national society must rest on a foundation of deep personal commitments to families, and strong families developed their coherence and continuity through a shared commitment to the nation. The possible conflicts between love of nation and love of family were downplayed in the popular images of ideal families nurturing future national citizens. Families were thus recognized (like schools) as crucial mediating institutions in which nationalist ideas could help shape the lives and commitments of each individual. The Italian nationalist Joseph Mazzini, for example, sought to link the idealized national and domestic family through images of a "home" that brought all Italians into a collective family network. "Our country is our home," Mazzini explained with a common domestic metaphor, "the home which God has given us, placing therein a numerous family which we love and are loved by, and with which we have a more intimate and quicker communion of feeling and thought than with others." This domestic national union was nevertheless threatened, like other families, by separations and distances that must be overcome in order for the national family to achieve the unity that all good families required. "As the members of a family cannot rejoice at the common table if one of their number is far away," Mazzini continued, ". . . so you should have no joy or repose as long as a portion of the territory upon which your language is spoken is separated from the Nation."[6] Such images of a lost or separated national "family" reappeared often in nationalist writings about still-unformed nation-states or about the territories that established nations had lost to other governments. In short, the emotional meaning of a grieving, divided, or united family could be invoked to support every call for national sacrifice and commitment. At the same time, however, Mazzini and other nationalists moved easily from these general metaphors of family identity into specific recommendations for individual behavior and personal domestic life, thus connecting nationalist ideologies to what might now be called "family values."

The rise of nationalism in the decades after the French Revolution coincided with the development of new ideas about the political significance of respectable families and sexual mores. Breaking with the old regime and reputed immorality of traditional aristocratic societies, the new leaders of sovereign nations promoted devotion to family and nation as the surest path to good morality and social order. This new alliance of moral reformers and nationalists has been described by the historian George Mosse, who argues that nationalism "sanctioned middle-class manners and morals and played a crucial part in spreading respectability to all classes of the population." Nationalist writers thus contributed to a wider bourgeois aspiration for well-regulated sexual behavior by praising marriage as the only appropriate venue for sexual relations and by advocating sexual restraint as the model for virtuous, "manly" national behavior. "Manliness meant freedom from sexual passion," Mosse explains, "the sublimation of sensuality into leadership of society and the nation." To be sure, this notion of sublimated sensuality was most pronounced in the Protestant cultures of northern Europe, but Mosse argues that concepts of manliness became linked more generally with the whole idea of a strong nation—in contrast to women and weak or "abnormal" men.

There could of course be no nation without women, yet the women came to represent the "passive" and "immutable" element of national societies. Men acted, used their reason for public causes, and made history; women embodied the deep, unchanging, natural force of the nation and made babies. Although women were responsible for the eternal moral values that respectable families and nations passed on to their children, they entered public life as symbols of timeless national virtue rather than as actors in the political and social processes of a dynamic national history. "The female embodiments of the nation [e.g., Marianne, Germania] stood for eternal forces. They looked backward in their ancient armor and medieval dress. Woman as a preindustrial symbol suggested innocence and chastity, a kind of moral rigor directed against modernity."[7] Placed on the pedestal of national purity, idealized national women were unable to participate in most of the political, social, and military institutions that represented and directed public life in the new national states; indeed, they were not even allowed to vote until the twentieth century.

Despite these restrictions on their public action, women loomed large in the nationalist imagination as the guardians of a crucial domestic sphere wherein boys and girls alike learned the meaning of their national culture. Weak families would therefore weaken the whole nation, whereas good, strong families created good, strong nations. The Polish nationalist Adam Mickiewicz described this family-nation connection as a system of mutual dependence and warned that domestic life suffered disruption and disorientation when national commitments and identities disappeared within families. National life must therefore overlap with family life, in Mickiewicz's view, and each family should share in the public goals of the nation while cultivating the memory of past national and family achievements. Women and men might have different roles in this nationalized family identity, and yet they fostered the same national and familial objectives.

> In the Middle Ages, the wife prayed in her chapel for the same cause that her husband fought for on the battlefield [Mickiewicz noted in a description of the ideal family]; she was certain that her prayers brought aid to her husband. They needed each other: working for the same goal, they felt united in the same spiritual work. The memories of dead parents continued to live among the children; they in-

Germania. Oil on canvas by Philipp Veit, 1835. Städelsches Kunstinstitut, Frankfurt am Main.

This painting by the German artist Philipp Veit portrays the symbolic meaning and unity of the nation as a woman. Seated on a throne with both rural and urban landscapes behind her, "Germania" holds a book, sword, and emblazoned shield as she ponders an imperial crown. This idealized woman evokes the tradition of a medieval Madonna, but Germania represents the sanctity of the nation rather than the sacred mother of Christ.

voked the memory of their mother as a saint and learned by
heart the history of their father.[8]

Unfortunately, Mickiewicz went on to explain, such shared commitments to a common goal and history no longer existed in most parts
of Europe, except in Poland, where "families still nourish within
themselves the great national life" and where even the wife "sometimes mounts a horse to defend the country."[9] Poland's national superiority therefore emerged for Mickiewicz in the strength of a distinctive family life that fused private memories with public causes
and personal religion with national aspirations. Other nationalists
claimed similar or different family virtues for their own nations, but
in almost every case the family stood at the mediating juncture
of private and public life. "To sanctify the Family more and more and
to link it ever closer to the Country," Mazzini reminded the Italians
in a typical nationalist summary of domestic duties; "this is your
mission."[10]

The widespread emphasis on the national significance of families
gave women an honorable, essential role in national life. Most nationalists assumed that women must be carefully prepared for their work
as guardians of family and national morality because their virtue provided the decisive first step in the education of the nation's children.
Yet the education of women, as most nationalists interpreted it, could
only build on those essential, immutable qualities that lay deep
within the nation's women and mothers. When Michelet wrote about
the need for national education in France, for example, he suggested
that the crucial early lessons could be learned in the homes of workers and artisans who already understood the domestic order that sustained a great nation. Michelet's account of working-class French
families in his book *The People* thus described the relationships between women and men that nationalists liked to portray as the vital,
creative source of successful national cultures. Returning home from
a day of hard work, the French working man finds his wife and children in the blissful surroundings of a simple home. "This woman is
virtue itself," Michelet explained in the language of nationalist gender stereotypes; she embodies "the particular charm of unaffected
reason and tact that enable her to govern strength without being
aware of it. This man is the strong, the patient, and courageous
[worker], who bears for society the heaviest load of human life." Indeed, Michelet explained that this weary French worker had to go off
to bed while his wife put the children to sleep and completed all the

domestic chores, because he must prepare himself for another day of labor in the world outside his home. "Early in the morning, long before he opens his eyes, she is up. Soon everything is ready—the warm food he eats at home and that which he takes with him. He goes off with his heart satisfied after kissing his wife and sleeping children, with no worries about what he is leaving."[11]

Michelet's flattering, idealized, male portrait of the happy French family thus emphasized the dichotomy of male and female labor, ascribed public action to men and domestic virtue to women, and placed the family at the center of a vibrant national life. Like many nationalists of the era, he complained about decadent aristocrats and bourgeois hedonists who did not follow the example of decent peasants and workers, but he had no doubt that the virtuous family embodied the deepest values of the virtuous French nation; and no task was more important to this family than the creation and education of the children who would become the citizens and inheritors of the nation.

Reproducing the Nation

Nationalist writers praised and worried about the family because this was the institution that produced and shaped the nation's children. The all-important biological labor in this institution depended of course on women, whose service to the nation was analogous to the mostly male labor of historians and writers. National cultures could only survive and flourish through a well-cultivated collective memory of the nation's past heroes and achievements, but there could be no national future without the constant reproduction of citizens. Men therefore took care of the nation's memory and current public problems, while women took care of the nation's biological survival. As Mazzini explained it, the woman's national duty was to "create the future . . . of which the living symbol is the child, link between us and the generations to come. Through her the Family, with its divine mystery of reproduction, points to eternity."[12] National history provided the much desired immortality for people who had already died; children sustained the hope of national (and personal) immortality for those who were still alive.

The anxieties about death that contributed much of the emotional force to the fusion of religion and nationalism thus appeared also in the anxieties about reproduction, families, and children. Births and deaths—the ultimate boundaries in the lives of individuals—shaped the future and past meaning of nations as well as families, so even the most philosophical nationalists speculated on the mysteries and pleasures of childhood and child rearing. "What man of noble mind," Fichte asked rhetorically, ". . . does not earnestly wish to relive his own life in a new and better way in his children and his children's children, and to continue to live on this earth, ennobled and perfected in their lives, long after he is dead?" Fichte raised his question with reference to the specific perspectives of a father, but he was certain that children offered the essential path to immortality for all individuals and nations alike. National struggles were therefore always in some sense about the survival of the children. When the German Protestants fought to establish their new religion, for example, they were thinking about "the bliss of their children and of their grandchildren as yet unborn and of all posterity as yet unborn."[13] For Fichte and most other nationalists, children and the "yet unborn" were the highest justification for every national sacrifice, including war and campaigns for national independence.

Children were hence the most precious national resource, and the ultimate (genocidal) crime against any national society would be to kill its children. The death of children meant the death of a nation, whereas virtually every other national catastrophe could eventually be overcome through the survival of the children in whom a nation would continue to exist. Children were often described as the pure embodiment of national virtues (resembling in this respect a good soldier), and images of happy or endangered children became common in nationalist writings and art. As Michelet noted in one of his warm evocations of French virtues, "The child is the people themselves in their native truth before they are deformed; it is the people without vulgarity, rudeness, or envy." Indeed, no matter what problems or setbacks might afflict the French, the children brought them back to their most profound national realities and national obligations. "In the name of our children," Michelet reminded his French readers, "we must not allow our country to perish."[14] The rhetorical invocation of children thus resembled the invocation of forefathers in nationalist literature and speeches, because children (like ancestors) seemed to carry the nation's virtue and original innocence. Even the most innocent and virtuous young people, however, still had to learn about the meaning of the nation in their schools and families.

The family was therefore a site of cultural reproduction as well as biological reproduction, and it gave women a cultural labor to complement their biological work. Like Adam Mickiewicz, who claimed superiority for Polish families on the grounds that they best sustained the memory of national accomplishments, nationalists everywhere called for a domestic cultural training that would ensure a deep national consciousness in every child. In this respect, as in so many others, the Italian writer Mazzini summarized the almost universal nationalist preoccupation with a kind of national "home schooling." Stressing the profound responsibility of all parents, Mazzini explained that "the task of the family is to educate *citizens*. Family and Country are the two extreme points of the same line. And where this is not so the Family degenerates into egoism." The successful, virtuous family celebrated its connection to a wider national community and gave the most conscientious attention to the children's understanding of their national identity. Take the children on your knee, Mazzini advised his compatriots, and "speak to them of their Country, of what it was, of what it ought to be." Children could learn these national truths better from their parents than from anybody else, but only if they heard constantly about their own place in a long history of ancestors. "Tell them over again the great deeds of the common people in our ancient republics," Mazzini implored; "teach them the names of the good men who loved Italy and her people, and endeavoured through suffering, calumny, and persecution to improve their destinies." The ideal national family thus helped each child understand his or her own intimate connection to the past in order to generate committed national actions in the future. Mazzini's authentic national family would always be united by personal love, yet the best parents would also make the family "a temple in which you may sacrifice together to the country."[15]

The nationalist concerns about children, reproduction, and families often led to an interest in sexual behaviors, which carried many nationalists beyond the problems of education into evolving debates about sexual mores and gender roles. Most nationalists regarded "nonproductive" sexual activity as a threat to national life—an idea for which they found confirmation in new medical literatures on the dangers of homosexuality, masturbation, and sexual promiscuity.[16] Nationalisms celebrated well-regulated heterosexuality, and homosexuals could only be deemed "abnormal" within ideologies that praised "good" citizens for marrying, producing children, and fostering national identities in their domestic relations. Even late marriages caused concern among some nationalists who worried that such marriages produced fewer children. Reflecting on the population in France (a country in which declining birth rates generated

Russian Loyalty and Heroism. Etching and aquatint, hand-colored by Clark and Dubourgh, after I. A. Atkinson, 1816. From the copy in the Rare Book Collection, The University of North Carolina, Chapel Hill.

Nationalist accounts of the family emphasized the importance of teaching children about heroes whose actions defended the honor of their nation. This etching conveys such nationalist themes with the image of a Russian father severing his own hand as he resists orders to help the French advance on Moscow in 1812. The child sees his father's heroism, which is required for the defense of his mother and for the future of his people. Although this English work portrays a Russian scene, its message of sacrifice appeared in all nationalist movements.

early and enduring nationalist concern), Michelet urged the bourgeoisie to marry at a younger age and to seek partners among the more vital lower classes. "That is the path to strength, beauty, and a bright future," Michelet told his readers. "Our young men marry late, already worn out, and generally take a sickly young lady. Their children die or live in poor health. After two or three generations our bourgeoisie will be as puny as our nobility before the Revolution." The national struggle of life against death, in short, posed new challenges for every generation, though the biological threats always appeared to be most dangerous in the cities. Michelet and many other nationalists in fact extended their anxieties about sexuality into a wider anxiety about national degeneration as the (imagined) hardy, rural populations moved from the countryside into new urban centers. "Not only is the body failing," Michelet noted in his warnings to the French bourgeoisie, "but so is the mind."[17]

Although Michelet did not push his commentaries on reproduction and families toward a detailed discussion of "race" and "blood," other writers began to speculate on the complex intersection of sex, families, and racial identities as they worried about degeneration or national purity. The status of women was also crucial in more race-conscious forms of nationalism, because a nation whose women "fell" to the men of other nations was a nation at risk of losing its national identity. National soldiers were thus portrayed as protectors of the nation's women, and national enemies in war became a menace to the nation's biological foundation as well as its politics or culture; indeed, violation of the nation's women represented (like the murder of children) an ultimate assault on the sanctity and survival of the nation. In the United States, for example, one of the most popular genres of national writing took the form of "captivity narratives" about European women who were taken prisoner by Indians. Portraying the "savage" as a sexual threat to European American women, these stories helped establish an American national identity along the boundaries of race, culture, and sexual behavior.[18]

Similar anxieties about sexual violation or racial mixing also appeared in European nationalist descriptions of warfare, overseas colonies, and threats of foreign invasion. Such fears surfaced dramatically in France when German soldiers poured across the Rhine in 1870 and 1914, threatening French women and the French nation with a sexual assault as well as a military occupation. Writers and artists in France portrayed the German seizure of French territory in the Franco-Prussian War as a literal and figurative rape of French mothers and "Mother" France, and French nationalists would emphasize the brutal, sexual aggression of German soldiers throughout World War I.[19] The biological reproduction of nations thus seemed to be most endangered during wars, but nationalists also worried in peacetime about sexual behaviors, national-minded child rearing, and the domestic responsibilities of women. Meanwhile, the biological themes in the nationalist writing about families became even more prominent in the growing nationalist concern with race.

Racial Theories and Nationalist Identities

Theories about the racial differences that separated nations developed somewhat later than the nationalist theories about distinctive national histories, political institutions, religions, and languages. Beginning in the 1840s and 1850s, however, nationalists increasingly turned to new biological sciences and pseudosciences to support their claims for unique national characteristics. Biological conceptions of national identities spread rapidly after the appearance of Charles Darwin's book *On the Origin of Species* (1859), and the subsequent development of Social Darwinism in European and American cultures provided ideological support for a new wave of nationalist imperialism. Some historians argue that the new biological theories evolved into forms of racism that differed in fundamental ways from nationalism. For example, whereas nationalists might stress the political will and history of a sovereign people, racists would stress physical or biological traits that existed outside of history, political institutions, or literary traditions. For many nationalists, though, the racial traits of a national population both shaped and reflected specific national histories.

This distinction between nationalism and racism often influences the historical dichotomies that are used to distinguish Western (political) nationalisms from Eastern (racial, ethnic) nationalisms, yet some of the most influential racist theories actually appeared first among English and French writers. Although Fichte's *Addresses to the German Nation* referred to the "Teutonic race," he generally described racial differences according to language—stressing the contrasts between the "living" German language and the "stagnant" or "derivative" languages of other European nations.[20] There was of course much racism in various strands of German nationalism by the late nineteenth century, but the German nationalist historian Friedrich Meinecke (who suggested that the existence of a nation required a "blood relationship") was still arguing in the early twentieth century that "there are no racially pure nations."[21]

The most complete expression of racist nationalism would emerge in the doctrines and policies of German Nazism, which transformed race into the central feature of all national identities. Was Nazism a nationalism or an extreme form of racism? This question remains a much debated issue, in part because defenders of nationalism in Germany and elsewhere insist that the racist, genocidal policies of the Nazis went far beyond the typical beliefs and policies of modern nationalisms. Although many familiar nationalist themes existed in

Nazi propaganda, "races" tended to replace "nations" when Nazis set out to explain historical conflicts and cultures. The Nazi ideologist Alfred Rosenberg, for example, assumed that racial struggles and identities were the guiding force in every nation's beliefs and actions. "Each race has its soul," Rosenberg wrote in 1930, "and each soul belongs to a race. . . . History no longer means war of class against class nor of church dogma and dogma, but blood and blood, race and race. . . . The race-bound national soul is the measure of all our thoughts, aspirations of will and deeds, the final criterion of our values. . . ."[22] Such racist thinking had catastrophic consequences when it became the reigning political theory in twentieth-century Europe's most powerful nation-state, and it may be difficult to examine the racial theories in nineteenth-century nationalisms when we know the horrific, violent history of racism and racist nationalism in Nazi Germany (and in other modern imperialisms). It would be inaccurate and unfair to describe all nineteenth-century ideas about race as "proto-Nazi" ideologies, but it is important to recognize that racial theories influenced most nationalisms of the era, even in nations whose nationalisms seemed to emphasize politics and history more than ethnicity and race.

Racial theories offered nationalist writers an apparently scientific perspective for characterizing the national cultures they wanted to define. Drawing on Enlightenment traditions that categorized natural phenomena according to various "objective" criteria, analysts identified the racial traits of different nationalities and ascribed social or intellectual qualities to physical differences. Among the early leaders in this new racial theorizing, the English writer Robert Knox (1791–1862) emerged as a popular lecturer and advocate for racial interpretations of world history. "The results of the physical and mental qualities of a race are naturally manifested in its civilization," Knox assured the readers of his book *The Races of Men* (1850), "for every race has its own form of civilization." This historical truth could be seen clearly in England, where the population was divided between the "Saxons" and the "Normans." The latter were a French "Celtic" race that had conquered England in the eleventh century (the "greatest calamity that ever befel England—perhaps, the human race," Knox complained), but the hardy Saxon qualities of old England could never be destroyed. The Saxons were "thoughtful, plodding, [and] industrious beyond all other races," Knox reported, and they were a remarkably "tall, powerful, athletic race of men; the strongest, as a race, on the earth;" indeed, they were the "only absolutely fair race on the face of the globe."[23] Equally important for Knox, these strong Saxon "men" loved freedom and abhorred feudalism, thereby distinguishing themselves from the Celtic (French) deference to chiefs and social elites.

This Celtic racial trait of obedience ran so deep in the French soul that even their most dramatic revolutionary demands for freedom always ended simply with deference to a new chief (e.g., Napoleon). "The world thought Celtic France a great and free people," Knox wrote in a commentary on the French Revolution, but "the world forgot the element of race . . . [in] the probable destinies of the French Celt."[24] Expressing their deepest racial instincts, the French preferred their military heroes over freedom and their Celtic deference over Saxon freedom. The whole course of French history was thus for Knox a perfect example of his theory: Political institutions and leaders might change over time, yet history could never transform habits that flowed from the essential nature of a race.

One could perhaps dismiss Knox and his absurd racial theories as historically insignificant, but his images of Saxon strength and freedom became a popular theme in much nineteenth-century writing about England and America. Many white Americans took racial pride in their historical links to Saxon England, thus giving English authors like Robert Knox a market on both sides of the Atlantic. When Ralph Waldo Emerson wrote *English Traits,* for example, he read Knox's racial theories and found himself referring to race as he pursued his subject. Despite his skepticism about Knox's racial absolutisms, Emerson noted that "it is in the deep traits of race that the fortunes of nations are written," and he portrayed the English as "more intellectual than other races." This intellectual superiority explained why the English nation tended to "assimilate other races to themselves," and why other peoples who came in contact with the English generally deferred to English dominance and learned the English language. Yet Emerson also suspected that England's dominance might be ending, that the nation had entered "her old age," and that the most dynamic activity of the "British race" might well be found on the plains and mountains of America rather than on the ancient island itself. Like aging parents, Emerson concluded, the English could find their future glory and strength in their American "children," whose "elasticity" would become the "hope of mankind" if or when the "old race" lost its expansive energy in Britain.[25]

Such comments do not make Emerson a racist or a racial determinist like Knox, but they do indicate how the language of race influenced both the English and American conceptions of national identity. Indeed, even before Knox and Emerson were writing about the Saxon and English races, the American historian George Bancroft (1800–1891) had used racial explanations to account for certain aspects of early American history. Developing sharp contrasts between the Native Americans and the English settlers who displaced them, Bancroft stressed that the Indians, "naked and feeble compared with the Europeans," could not possibly match the Europeans in civilized skills or military prowess. To be sure, he saw in the Indians a common humanity, but their racial differences seemed to have more historical influence than the deeper human qualities they shared with "Caucasians." Bancroft's narrative of America's emerging national culture thus established clear distinctions between the "races" on the North American continent and showed why racial differences helped the "Caucasians" to prevail. Descended from "that Germanic race most famed for the love of personal independence," the "Anglo-Saxons" had carried their traditional racial strengths into the remote forests of America. "The Anglo-Saxon mind," Bancroft explained, "in its serenest nationality, . . . fondly cherishing the active instinct for personal freedom . . . and legislative power . . . had made its dwelling-place in the empire of Powhatán."[26]

As for the Indians, Bancroft argued that they could not respond creatively to the intrusions from Europe because "the red man has aptitude at imitation rather than invention." Although the Indian could think about objects, he lacked the "faculty of abstraction to lift himself out of the dominion of his immediate experience . . . and he is inferior in reason and the moral qualities." Some sympathetic observers might assume that such flaws appeared only in certain individuals, but Bancroft reported that "this inferiority" was in fact "the characteristic of the race."[27] Bancroft was a strong Jacksonian Democrat who celebrated the virtues of political equality, and yet his popular narrative of American history rested on various racial assumptions that made the conquest (or death) of the Native American population easier for European Americans to accept and understand.

Like many other nationalisms of the era, Bancroft's expansive vision of America's destiny presumed a racial hierarchy and placed his own favorite racial category ("Anglo-Saxon") in a privileged historical position. He was by no means a proto-Nazi, but his support for America's national expansion clearly expressed influential, popular forms of racism. Similar racist theories were also used in this same era to exclude both free and enslaved Africans from the social and political rights of American national citizenship, and most European Americans viewed the nation's essential identity as the political, cultural, and economic expression of the white (or "Anglo-Saxon") race. The growing racial consciousness in nineteenth-century Western culture spread across both Europe and North America, but the most comprehensive summary of the ostensible links between races and nations may have appeared in the works of the French writer Arthur de Gobineau. A long-time critic of the French Revolution and of subsequent movements for democratic political reforms, Gobineau developed a racial explanation for France's past achievements and recent problems in a book called *Essay on the Inequality of the Human Races* (1853–1855). Although he was a contemporary of Knox and other racial theorists, Gobineau was more concerned with the decline of races and nations than with the limitless possibilities for future racial achievements. He therefore helped launch a new form of racialist writing that emphasized the national dangers of mixing races (the themes here did begin to resemble the ideas of twentieth-century Nazism), the decisive influence of race in all spheres of history, and the consequences of what he called racial degeneration. "The word *degenerate*," Gobineau wrote, "when applied to a people, means . . . that the people has no longer the same intrinsic value as it had before, because it has no longer the same blood in its veins, continual adulterations having gradually affected the quality of that blood. In other words, though the nation bears the name given by its founders, the name no longer connotes the same race."[28]

The meaning of a nation for Gobineau was thus inseparable from the purity of its "blood"—an alleged historical fact that posed grave problems for old nations in which generations of racial "mixing" had transformed the original population. "So long as the blood and institutions of a nation keep to a sufficient degree the impress of the original race," Gobineau argued, "that nation exists." This imagined racial purity provided the only secure defense against assaults on the nation's ancient institutions, yet the most powerful nations were also the most vulnerable to the racial mixing that would cause their decline. Strong nations tended to conquer less powerful peoples, whereupon the fateful processes of racial mixing immediately began to weaken the conquering nation. "From the very day when the conquest is accomplished and the fusion begins," Gobineau explained in a typical generalization, "there appears a noticeable change of quality in the blood of the masters."[29] Since "mixed" nations inevitably lost their vitality and strength, Gobineau assumed that Europe's once-pure nations would gradually decline and that racial mixing in the United States would undermine its national growth and power.

Gobineau's historical conception of national accomplishments and decline rested on typical racist theories about racial traits and racial hierarchies. Predictably enough, he placed the northern "white" European race at the top of a racial pyramid that descended steadily down toward the populations of America, Africa, and Asia. Developing some of the most extreme historical claims of the era, Gobineau told his readers that "all civilizations derive from the white race, that none can exist without its help, and that a society is great and brilliant only so far as it preserves the blood of the noble group that created it." Such theories fit comfortably with European assumptions about their own imperialist projects, the growing belief in biological causality, and the pretensions of European social elites, but they also suggested the dangers that Gobineau saw lurking in France and other European nations. The expanding power of the "white" race was also expanding the racial mixtures that destroyed national traditions and creativity. "This [racial mixing] will lead eventually to mediocrity in all fields," Gobineau warned, "mediocrity of physical strength, mediocrity of beauty, mediocrity of intellectual capacities."[30]

Gobineau's pessimism about his nation's future diverged from the usual optimism of nineteenth-century nationalists, most of whom saw their nations' distinctive "racial" traits as the foundation for future expansion and influence. In fact, few nationalists went as far as Gobineau or Knox in stressing the racial essence of national identities, though they commonly attributed at least some of their nation's achievements to superior racial traits such as "physical strength" or "intelligence" or "love of freedom." Extreme theories of racial determinism, however, did not give enough attention to the individual choices and historical agency that most liberal nationalists invoked to rally their compatriots to political action and national causes. Gobineau's pessimism thus anticipated another kind of fin de siècle nationalism in France and elsewhere that focused obsessively on the dangers of national decline instead of the prospects for exceptional national progress.

The Belief in National Exceptionalism

Nineteenth-century nationalists drew on the prestige of the new biological sciences to reinforce ideas about distinctive national identities that had already developed in historical studies, philology, literary criticism, and religious rituals. Long-term continuities in the "nature" of women and men, the relations within families, and the racial traits of national populations seemed to express and embody the inherent virtues of nations and the distinctive characteristics that separated each nation from all others. Although the meaning of gender, family, and race evolved through the same cultural systems that constructed the meaning of history, literature, and religion, nationalists typically praised the immutable qualities of women, children, and "manly" citizens as the transparent, transcendental, or natural essence of national identities.

These apparently natural attributes nevertheless had to be cultivated in homes and schools that taught young people how their various gender roles, racial characteristics, and social obligations merged with the history of their nation. All nationalists wanted to link collective, public identities with the emerging personal identities of children through a constant immersion in the nation's history, language, and traditions. Parents would thus extend the work of schools into their homes by teaching the public lessons of national identity to the rising generation, including the lesson that each child was fortunate to have been born into a unique national family. This theme of national exceptionalism runs through every nationalist ideology, in part because the belief in national identity and difference almost invariably rested on claims for national superiority in language, politics, culture, religion, or race. When people believed that their nation embodied the highest level of achievement in some or many spheres of human civilization, they also assumed that the history of their own nation took on universal significance and that the survival or expansion of their own national population carried consequences for the whole world. The themes of biology and history came together on this point because the constant reproduction of future generations was of course the essential precondition for any nation that was entrusted with world-historical destinies and duties.

The belief in national exceptionalism drew on old religious ideas about chosen peoples, but it took on new intensity when it merged with biological metaphors of birth and death, growth and degeneration. No matter how much a nation's specific public issues, enemies, and conflicts might evolve across time, nationalists could always use the exceptionalism of their nation's history or mission to justify renewed national commitment and action. Fichte's call for action against Napoleon, for example, portrayed the struggle as a test for all of humanity. "You of all modern peoples," Fichte assured his German audience, "[are] the one in whom the seed of human perfection most unmistakably lies, and to whom the lead in its development is committed. If you perish ... then there perishes together with you every hope of the whole human race for salvation from the depths of its miseries. . . . If you go under, all humanity goes under with you, without hope of any future restoration."[31] Whereas historical realists might have described Germany's conflict with France as simply another episode in a long struggle for resources and territory, the nationalist philosopher interpreted the German cause as a campaign for the entire future of humanity. It was of course a huge responsibility—the development of this "seed of human perfection"—yet it was also in Fichte's view a decisive opportunity for the Germans to show their unique commitment to the most elevated human aspirations for freedom and salvation.

Across the Rhine, however, nineteenth-century French nationalists conceded nothing to the Germans when it came to claiming exceptional national destinies. Michelet's commentaries on French history and the French people constantly proclaimed France's universal significance (mirroring in this respect Fichte's claims for Germany) and located the whole course of world history in the victories and defeats of the French nation. Describing this extraordinary nation as "the salvation of mankind," Michelet wrote proudly that "the national legend of France is an immense unbroken stream of light, a veritable Milky Way which the world has always fixed its eyes upon." The universal interest in French achievements was of course a great honor, yet it also produced exceptional obligations because the world could be "lost perhaps for a thousand years if France succumbs" to those who opposed or ignored its unique national history.[32] Michelet's concluding calls for national action in *The People* thus repeated in French the same apocalyptic, quasi-religious assumptions about human salvation that Fichte had developed earlier in Germany. In both cases, the nation became a kind of mediating messiah for people everywhere. "The fatherland, my fatherland," Michelet wrote, "can alone save the world."[33]

A long century of such writings about exceptional national missions helps explain why the national hatreds were much stronger in the French-German war of 1914 to 1918 than they had been in the French-German wars of the Napoleonic era, but it would be wrong to assume that grandiose claims for world-historical nations appeared only in the heated imaginations of European intellectuals. The modern discourse of national exceptionalism and chosen peoples emerged very early in the history of America ("the city on a hill"), and American confidence in a unique national destiny only grew stronger during the century after the American Revolution. By the end of the nineteenth century the United States was claiming its place as one of the major imperial nations of the world, though some Americans worried about whether they should take control of people in distant lands such as the Philippines. Responding to these doubts in the first month of 1900, Senator Albert Beveridge (1826–1927) of Indiana delivered a speech on America's exceptional destiny in which he justified the colonization of the Philippines and asserted the national claims for America that Fichte and Michelet had long since made for their countries in Europe.

Beveridge believed that the need for American expansion was a "racial" question because God had made the "English-speaking and Teutonic peoples" the talented "master organizers of the world." More specifically, "He has made us adept in government that we may administer government among savage and senile peoples. . . . And of all our race He has marked the American people as His chosen nation to finally lead in the regeneration of the world. This is the divine mission of America, and it holds for us all the profit, all the glory, all the happiness possible to man. We are the trustees of the world's progress."[34] Americans had always believed in the uniqueness of their national calling, so an American nationalist hardly needed the European intellectual contributions of Fichte, Michelet, Mazzini, Mickiewicz, Knox, or Gobineau to claim an exceptional mission for the United States. Yet Senator Beveridge repeated many of the most common themes in the racial nationalisms of late-nineteenth-century Western culture as he evoked images of senility, regeneration, and the "divine mission" of a "chosen nation" to advocate an American occupation of the Philippines.

The earlier political and religious conceptions of American exceptionalism had by no means disappeared during the nineteenth century, but the nationalism of Senator Beveridge and many other Americans resembled the nationalisms of other cultures in more ways than the historical dichotomies of "Western" and "Eastern" nationalisms suggest. American nationalists, like their European counterparts, drew on biology, worried about families and gender roles, promoted racial stereotypes, and affirmed the unique natural and historical qualities of their national society. Placed in the wider context of European nationalist ideas, the emergence and cultural evolution of American nationalism tends to exemplify rather than differ from the ideological assumptions of most modern nationalisms.

6

The Cultural Construction of Nationalism in Early America

Earlier chapters of this book argue that nationalism has always grown out of specific cultural histories and that the nationalisms in Europe and America had more similarities than the traditional dichotomies of "Western" and "Eastern" nationalisms suggest. These general claims could be explored and debated with a wide range of historical examples in Europe and America, but the emergence of nationalism in the early history of the United States offers an excellent, exemplary case for more detailed analysis of both the recurring cultural themes of Western nationalisms and the overlapping currents of nationalist thought on both sides of the Atlantic. Americans managed to construct a national identity and nationalist ideology quite rapidly in the decades between their break from Britain (1776) and their painful, bloody Civil War (1861–1865), so their early national history shows how a diverse, scattered population could be "narrated" into a nation in political institutions, schools, religious rituals, public celebrations, family memories, literature, and history books. This final chapter therefore returns to various aspects of modern nationalist ideology through the writings of three authors who contributed significantly to the evolving narratives in which Americans invented their national traditions and imagined their nation: the poet Philip Freneau (1752–1832), the historian George Bancroft (1800–1891), and President Abraham Lincoln (1809–1865).

The new American nation's lack of ancient history, unique language, or exclusive ethnic identity pushed the American search for national distinctiveness toward politics, religion, geography, economic prosperity, and domestic virtue. At the same time, however, there was a strong racial component in early American nationalism because the "true" American had to be distinguished from both the Native American race (whose land was taken) and the African race (whose civil rights were completely denied in slavery). American nationalists thus constructed their ideology by emphasizing two cultural and political themes that could be found in virtually every nationalist movement of the era: They assumed that the United States had a unique destiny or mission in world history, and they assumed that this destiny was manifested in the differences that separated America from the world's other nations and peoples and systems of government. American exceptionalism presumed that the United States had broken decisively with Old World values and institutions, but it also emphasized fundamental differences that divided European Americans from Native Americans, who were of course the truly ancient Americans.

Historians have long pointed to the religious character of early American claims for a unique national mission. Drawing on the Bible and a deep sense of Puritan moral rectitude, Americans saw themselves (especially in New England) as the Chosen People from whom God expected the highest human virtues and to whom he promised a unique, decisive political and religious influence on the future history of the world.[1] Religious leaders frequently referred to this God-given mission in sermons that interpreted American victories or defeats during the Revolutionary War as part of God's plan for the emerging nation (see chapter 4), but the belief in America's divine destiny remained as strong among nineteenth-century nationalists as it had been among the eighteenth-century ministers. When the editor of *The United States Magazine and Democratic Review*, John Sullivan, summarized America's identity in the late 1830s, for example, he was certain that the divine will could be discerned everywhere. "We are the nation of human progress . . . ," Sullivan assured the readers of his magazine, "Providence is with us. . . . We point to the everlasting truths on the first page of our national declaration. . . . In its magnificent domain of space and time, the nation of many nations is destined to manifest to mankind the excellence of divine principles."[2]

Such themes echoed through political speeches, newspaper editorials, poems, and novels, thereby encouraging Americans in every region and economic condition to believe that they lived in God's favorite nation. Readers of Herman Melville's novel *White-Jacket* (1850), for instance, came across the following summary of America's exceptional national destiny in a passage on the evils of flogging sailors:

> We Americans are the peculiar, chosen people—the Israel of our time; we bear the ark of the liberties of the world. . . . God has predestinated, mankind expects, great things from our race. . . . We are the pioneers of the world; the advance-guard, sent on through the wilderness of untried things, to break a new path in the New World that is ours. In our youth is our strength; in our inexperience our wisdom.[3]

Although Melville later developed a more skeptical view of American national culture, his novel in 1850 expressed some of the most prominent themes in the contemporary nationalist ideology, including confident assertions that the New World differed profoundly from the Old World and that God wanted this New World to belong to the advancing European Americans.

American conceptions of a divinely ordained national mission contributed to a widely held belief that the new nation's cultural and political differences from the Old World also made it morally superior. In contrast to the hierarchies, corruptions, and despotisms of European aristocrats, cities, and kings, nationalist orators explained, Americans were building a more virtuous society on the foundation of social equality, public honesty, and political democracy. This simple dichotomy of "Old" corruptions and "New" virtues shaped American self-images throughout the revolutionary war against Britain and the subsequent era of France's revolutionary and Napoleonic wars, which culminated for the Americans in another war with Britain. The War of 1812 aroused strong opposition as well as fervent nationalist enthusiasm, but the nationalist account of the conflict constantly reiterated the contrast between a peace-loving, democratic America and a belligerent, aristocratic Britain. The English symbolized anti-American, Old World hostilities that seemed to persist and even grow after the Americans had established their own successful institutions and economy. Complaining about the British arrogance toward America, one Congressman from Kentucky summarized the English threat that seemed forever to separate the United States from dangerous enemies across the sea. "This deep rooted [American] enmity to Great Britain arises from her insidious policy, the offspring of her perfidious conduct towards the United States," Richard Johnson argued in a Congressional speech. "Her disposition is unfriendly; her enmity is implacable; she sickens at our prosperity and happiness."[4] It was of course difficult to defeat this jealous, haughty enemy, but the very intensity of the struggle gave Americans a strong sense of their difference from Europeans and a deep pride in their national victories. "The proudest people in the world," one editorialist reported in a commentary (1815) on America's war with the British, "have been met and defeated, single-handed too, by a nation they had affected to despise."[5] This desire to affirm American triumphs over England's military and political power suggests how the emerging national identity depended on a deep sense of the differences and superiority that appeared in American narratives about conflicts with the Old World. Indeed, for most Americans, isolation from European societies, ideas, and wars became the surest protection for American virtues and institutions.

Yet the American nationalists had to do more than simply separate the United States from Europe, because they were equally engaged on their Western frontier with Indians who claimed "American" lands as their own territory. The cultural defense of American distinctiveness thus drew clear boundaries both inside and outside the North American continent and then defined the national superiority in each case by emphasizing the characteristics of national difference. Whereas the American nationalist narrative about Europe stressed the dangers of an aging, corrupt civilization, the descriptions of Native Americans developed a different dichotomy of civilization (now identified as American) and savagery that inevitably placed the savage behavior on the other side of the frontier. Ironically enough, when Americans fought with Indians they linked themselves to European cultures that they otherwise condemned in their political and cultural declarations of independence. As the writer Timothy Flint explained during a period of intense hostility toward (and forced removal of) Native Americans in the early 1830s, the blame for frontier conflicts lay entirely on the side of "uncivilized" Indians, who "were not sufficient civilians to distinguish between the right of empire and the right of soil." No compromise could be arranged with such people, Flint argued, because their institutions and beliefs were completely alien to the good sense of progress and civilization: "Our industry, fixed residences, modes, laws, institutions, schools, [and] religions rendered a union with them as incompatible as with animals of another nature." This deep incompatibility meant that the United States must displace the entire Native American population, and yet this vast assault on the Indians should be understood as part of God's unfolding plan. "In the unchangeable order of things," wrote Flint, "two such races can not exist together, each preserving a co-ordinate identity. Either this great continent, in the order of Providence, should have remained in the occupancy of half a million of savages, . . . or it must have become, as it has, the domain of civilized millions."[6] Flint did not use the term "manifest destiny" (the phrase did not appear until 1845), but the nationalist ideology that justified American expansion had long since established the reigning assumption that Indians could never hold legitimate claims to lands that Providence had reserved for the United States.

Popular nationalist accounts of America's destiny and cultural achievements thus shaped a powerful, reassuring national identity for a new nation that was defining itself against other people in both the Old World and the New. The new nation's unity nevertheless faced constant threats from the enormous geographical space, the rivalries of different regions, the constant influx of new immigrants, the relative weakness of the national government, and the growth of a rival, southern nationalism in the mid–nineteenth century. New narratives about America's national identity, unity, and history were therefore needed in every decade to retell the story of a national future and past that would justify continuing personal commitment and action. The nationalist writers who told these stories celebrated the political accomplishments of America and wrote endlessly about the nation's cultural accomplishments, its religious devotion to God or to deceased heroes, and its domestic virtues or racial strengths. This vast literature took every conceivable form of cultural expression and flourished in more cultural contexts than even the most comprehensive historical account could fully describe, but the writings of Freneau, Bancroft, and Lincoln offer some of the best examples of the key nationalist themes in poetry and prose.

Philip Freneau's American Future

Philip Freneau grew up in New Jersey, attended college at Princeton, and spent the years of the American Revolution as a merchant seaman, a member of the New Jersey militia, a temporary prisoner on a British prison ship, and a poet. Following the war, he continued to write poems about America, but he also became a journalist and later edited *The National Gazette,* a Jeffersonian newspaper that was published in Philadelphia during the early 1790s. Many of his poems and newspaper articles were collected in various books, including *The Poems of Philip Freneau* (1786), *The Miscellaneous Works of Philip Freneau* (1788), and *Letters on Various Interesting and Important Subjects* (1799). Although much of his work reflected journalistic haste or the passing political issues of the day, Freneau's writing provided important, early definitions of American national identity and attracted respectful support from national leaders such as Thomas Jefferson and James Madison.[7] He was, in short, a typical nationalist narrator who described America's unique political achievements, stressed the national differences from Europe, praised the revolutionary dead with a quasi-religious reverence, and compared the virtuous domestic lives of humble Americans with the alleged decadence of English aristocrats.

The two central themes of Freneau's political commentaries celebrated the brilliance of America's revolutionary political leaders and the nation's unparalleled commitment to human freedom and popular sovereignty. Like every American nationalist of his own time and later, Freneau portrayed George Washington as a uniquely talented, virtuous commander whose personal traits placed him in the highest rank of world-historical heroes and whose extraordinary resistance to British tyranny gave him a saintly status among his compatriots in the emerging American nation. "What few presum'd, you boldly atchiev'd / ," Freneau wrote in 1781, "A tyrant humbled, and a world reliev'd."[8] Despite some later doubts about the policies of Washington's presidential administration, Freneau's praise for Washington remained a leitmotiv through all his nationalist poetry, thus contributing to the pride in the Founding Fathers that united Americans who otherwise disagreed on specific laws or public policies. At the time of Washington's death, for example, Freneau published the kind of eulogy that ensured the national "Father" his distinguished place in America's national ideology:

> O *Washington!* thy honoured dust,
> To Parent Nature we entrust;
> Convinc'd that thy exalted mind
> Still lives, but soars beyond mankind;
> Still acts in Virtue's sacred cause,
> Nor asks from man his vain applause.[9]

Washington was by no means the only national leader to earn Freneau's admiration (other poems praised the genius of Franklin and

Washington Giving the Laws to America. Etching and engraving, c. 1800.
Anonymous. McAlpin Collection. Miriam and Ira D. Wallach Division
of Art, Prints, and Photographs, The New York Public Library, Astor,
Lenox, and Tilden Foundation.

George Washington's status as a quasi-religious figure in American
nationalist thought emerges clearly in this etching. Serving his people as
a lawgiver who replicates the Biblical role of Moses, Washington offers a
working constitution and receives the acclaim of a united, emerging
nation. Early American nationalist rituals (e.g., Fourth of July
celebrations) routinely referred to Washington as the virtuous father of
the nation.

Jefferson), yet Washington seemed to stand above all his peers in defending the righteous cause of American independence. Washington thus became for Freneau "The brightest name on *Freedom's* page, / And the first Honour of our Age."[10]

Even the greatest general, however, could not win a battle without his troops, and Freneau was certain that America's common people had contributed as much as the famous national leaders to the nation's military and political achievements. Freneau insisted in his newspaper articles that Americans understood the meaning of freedom and national sovereignty more profoundly than any other people in the world. "In a free government," he explained, "every man is a king, every woman is a queen," which meant that America would never accept Old World hierarchies, privileges, or exclusions. Rejecting European prejudices, Americans proclaimed that "ALL MEN ARE BORN EQUALLY FREE" and thus refused to give special homage to royalty or ancient elites. This strong American preference for the sovereignty of equal people over the sovereignty of kings pointed toward the republican political systems of the future, all of which would reject the prerogatives of monarchs and their courtiers. As Freneau argued in a political poem of the early 1790s, *republican* America provided the best defense of human rights and the best hope for eventual world peace.

> Be ours the task, the ambitious to restrain,
> And this great lesson teach, That kings are vain,
> That warring realms to certain ruin haste,
> That kings subsist on war, and wars are waste;
> So shall our nation, form'd on Reason's plan,
> Remain the guardian of the Rights of man,
> A vast republic, fam'd thro' every clime,
> *Without a king, to see the end of time!*[11]

Freneau's poems often lacked political subtlety and aesthetic nuance, but they conveyed the story of America's political mission clearly enough to reach anyone who picked up a newspaper or anyone who wanted to know how America differed from the old monarchical states of Europe.

According to Freneau, American independence and virtue could flourish because the new nation was far removed from the European continent and cultures. Indeed, he joined with many Americans in celebrating the great width of an Atlantic Ocean that seemed to shield the New World from all the agonies of the Old: "Remov'd from Europe's feuds, a hateful scene / (Thank heaven, such wastes of ocean roll between)."[12] The cultural distance from Europe was no less significant than the geographical separation, however, and Freneau strongly believed that the cultural difference provided the most enduring protection of individual freedoms. Each stranger arrived in America to find a free land, "Where no proud despot holds him down, / No slaves insult him with a crown,"[13] but the freedom and sovereignty of America could only survive through steadfast opposition to the never-ending threat of England's royal and aristocratic subversions. This defense against Europe's aristocratic corruptions required permanent American vigilance because the nation's enemies never disappeared ("All Tyranny's engines again are at work, / To make you as poor and as base as the Turk"[14]), and yet Freneau seemed never to doubt that America's egalitarian principles would ultimately prevail.

America's future victories over European despotism would of course reflect the superiority of its political institutions, but these institutions also fostered an economic growth that became both the product of a free government and the foundation for future national power. Like most American nationalists, Freneau interpreted the nation's rapid economic development as a sign of its superior political and cultural institutions. Although America could still not challenge the cultural superiority of Europe's artists and poets, it could at least challenge Europeans in the economic spheres of agriculture, commerce, and trade. Freneau's vision of America's continuing rivalry with Europe thus included an imagined future in which the American economy reached unprecedented levels of prosperity and international influence.

> It is not easy to conceive what will be the greatness and importance of North America in a century or two to come, [Freneau wrote in the 1780s], if the present fabric of Nature is upheld, and the people retain those bold and manly sentiments of freedom, which actuate them at this day. Agriculture, the basis of a nation's greatness, will here, most probably, be advanced to its summit of perfection; and its attendant, commerce, will so agreeably and usefully employ mankind, that wars will be forgotten.[15]

Freedom would produce prosperity, and the subsequent development of America would show the whole world how republican government and economics could remove violence and warfare from human history. In the end, this American achievement would be recognized and embraced even in Europe, though it might take time " 'Til Europe, humbled, greets our western wave / And owns an equal—whom she wish'd a slave."[16]

America's economic growth and fertile land could thus be linked to the nation's military and political achievements to suggest a strong divine support for the future American development that Freneau liked to imagine. It was nevertheless important in Freneau's view to build this national future with reverent remembrance of people who had sacrificed their lives for the independence that had produced America's flourishing economic and political system. Some of his best poems therefore invoked memories of the dead as he reflected, for example, on English prison ships in which "the ardent brave / Too often met an early grave," or as he described old battlefields and cemeteries. Deaths in battle were not the same as other deaths, because soldiers were ensured an honorable immortality in the life of a grateful nation. "Ah, what is death, when fame like *this* endears, /" Freneau wrote in a poem about a soldier who had died in South Carolina, *"The brave man's favourite, and his country's tears."*[17] Freneau may have harbored Jeffersonian doubts about Christian conceptions of life after death, but he believed deeply in the nation's promise of immortality to all who died for its cause.

The life of the nation thus flourished in the continuing existence of a whole people, whose soul could be found in the domestic arrangements of daily life as well as the heroism on a battlefield. Indeed, the common people became national heroes in Freneau's account of the social traits that distinguished America from Europe. Unlike corrupt European nobles, Freneau noted in one of his articles, "our AMERICAN FARMERS are virtuous, not in name but in REALITY. Vice has not been able to entice them from the standard of VIRTUE, INDEPENDENCE, and FREEDOM." These virtuous farmers guarded America's rights, embodied America's dignity, and supported the national Constitution. America's virtue was thus ensured if the nation's leaders would continue to rely on such hardy people for political and cultural guidance, though of course this natural virtue would have to be encouraged and supported. Dangers lurked in the plots of European aristocrats and even in popular plays about the lives of kings. The ultimate survival of the national good sense was nevertheless protected by the common people's determined insistence that "AMERICA SHALL STILL BE FREE."[18]

The future held little promise, however, for the other people of America—the Indians who faced the endless, overwhelming expansion of the prosperous European American population. Freneau predicted in one of his commentaries that the Native Americans might in fact disappear from the continent, though he tried to show some sympathy for their plight by placing his reflections in the voice of an imaginary Indian king named Opay Mico. *"We* are a miserable people," he had Mico explain, "our numbers decreasing from year to year, and our country gradually contracting itself into a very small circle." Despite the fact that Mico could see what was happening, his people's decline was apparently beyond anyone's control, and the imaginary monologue ended with Mico's unhappy lament that his people would one day "be reckoned among the lost things of the world."[19] Freneau's description of this loss (published in 1790) suggested that America's progress toward a prosperous, republican future carried catastrophic costs for at least some of the world's people, yet his recognition of the Native American tragedy did not destroy his optimism. He once wrote a fanciful account of how people would be living in New York in 1940, for example, in which he portrayed a flourishing future city and civic life: George Washington would be the most esteemed historical figure, slavery would have been abolished, superstition would have disappeared, and religious tolerance would guarantee a peaceful harmony for all. There would also be merchants and traders from all nations of the world, except for the Native Americans, who had vanished from history.[20]

Such descriptions of an expansive national future became a common feature of nationalisms in the nineteenth century, so Freneau's imaginary future America represents an early example of the popular new narratives about the meaning of national time. Optimistic visions of the future could not really sustain a strong national identity, however, if they lacked a parallel narrative about the nation's past. Good nationalists always stressed that history provided the surest evidence of a nation's identity or mission, which may suggest why Freneau's optimism about America's future would be greatly expanded in Bancroft's confident, optimistic narrative about America's past.

George Bancroft's American Past

George Bancroft grew up in Massachusetts, graduated from Harvard, studied in Germany, became a state leader in the Democratic Party during the antebellum era, served as American ambassador to

England (1846–1849) and Germany (1867–1873), and also found time along the way to produce a steady stream of articles and books on politics, history, and culture.[21] His greatest contribution to the evolving narrative of American national identity appeared in his monumental, ten-volume *History of the United States, from the Discovery of the American Continent,* which was published over four decades between 1834 and 1874. Despite the title's reference to the "United States," the books actually dealt with the nation's emergence during the colonial and revolutionary era, ending with the British recognition of American independence in the early 1780s. The key point of Bancroft's massive work was thus to show the development of a political, cultural, and religious identity that had united the European Americans of the future United States in a heroic campaign for national independence. Bancroft expressed great confidence in America's progressive development, emphasized the growing separation from Old World institutions and ideas, and celebrated the emerging nation's independence with characteristic nationalist pride in its exceptional leaders, ideals, and virtues.

According to Bancroft, the essence of America lay in its energetic, freedom-loving people, whose sovereign will established the firm foundation for the nation's government and laws. Bancroft shared of course the typical nationalist respect for the individual Founding Fathers, and his praise for Washington placed America's most famous national "Father" above virtually every leader in world history. ("Never in the tide of time," Bancroft wrote, "has any man lived who had in so great a degree the almost divine faculty to command the confidence of his fellow-men and rule the willing."[22]) Yet even Washington and his many talented associates could not have succeeded without the widely shared love of freedom that flourished among the common people of America. The unique meaning of America's Revolution therefore developed in the popular movement for self-government, wherein "the equality of all men was declared; personal freedom secured in its complete individuality; and common consent recognized as the only just origin of fundamental laws."[23]

This respect for individual freedom and popular sovereignty separated America from Europe, because Europeans deferred to political and social hierarchies in which "power moved from a superior to inferiors and subjects."[24] If Europeans worried about what would happen when people acted freely to shape their own government, Bancroft offered complete assurance that democratic political principles in America had produced a rapidly growing population, an expand-

Washington Crossing the Delaware. Oil on canvas by Emanuel Leutze, 1851. The Metropolitan Museum of Art, Gift of John S. Kennedy, 1897.

This famous painting expresses the nationalist themes that George Bancroft and other writers reiterated in early nineteenth-century texts. The heroic Washington stands firm as he guides the ship of the new American nation across a treacherous river of obstacles and dangers, but he could not have made this trip without the unknown people who surround him and contribute their own sacrifices to the shared national cause.

ing economy, a strong system of education, and a lively free press—all of which made America "an asylum to the virtuous, the unfortunate, and the oppressed of every nation." Other societies were beginning to accept the new principles of self-government, Bancroft noted in the introduction to the first volume of his *History* (1834), but no other nation had gone nearly so far in accepting the central theme of American public life: "The sovereignty of the people is here a conceded axiom, and the laws, established upon that basis, are cherished with faithful patriotism."[25] Like most nationalists, Bancroft stressed the unity of this shared patriotism rather than the internal divisions or conflicts that emerged whenever Americans extended their political discussions from general pieties into debates about slavery or tariffs or government expenditures. Bancroft's description of unity and shared ideals thus offered valuable historical support for the belief in a coherent American national identity, which could not have survived if the reigning historical paradigm had stressed the differences in America's population or regions (southern nationalists would of course build their arguments on contrasting narratives about internal differences).

The unity and uniqueness of America became most apparent to Bancroft through comparisons with the politics and cultures of Europe. Although he frequently noted that Americans drew on earlier British conceptions of liberty to develop their own distinctive national faith, he insisted that such principles had never been fully developed or instituted until the Americans launched their new nation; indeed, the British turned against their own traditions when they sent their armies against the American patriots who "refused conformity to foreign laws and external rule." Americans had thus used "their vigorous vitality" to claim the freedom that the people of other nations could only dream about. "When all Europe slumbered over questions of liberty," America's hardy pioneers on the frontier of civilization took charge of their providential destiny. "They were not only able to govern themselves," Bancroft argued, "they alone were able to do so; subordination visibly repressed their energies."[26]

And what had been the consequences of this exceptional campaign for national freedom? Bancroft found the answer to that question in the astonishing achievements of early American society, which included remarkable economic growth, the financial solvency of government institutions, and the constant expansion into western territories. Where lands had long remained dormant in the hands of "feeble barbarians," the new American settlers quickly developed a flourishing agriculture and trade that carried the United States to "the first rank of nations" and attracted "an immense concourse of emigrants" from all the nations of Europe. Contrary to the expectations of monarchs in Old World societies, the new nation had retained its unity, defended its freedom, and become a model for the rest of the world. Americans in fact "possessed beyond any other portion of the world the great ideas of their age," Bancroft explained, and they had generously shared their ideas with anyone who would listen. The new truths of politics and society therefore flowed back to Europe, providing instruction and inspiration for people who had never understood how they could be free. "And the astonished nations," Bancroft reported, "as they read that all men are created equal, started out of their lethargy."[27]

America's world-historical contributions to the understanding and practice of human freedom reflected for Bancroft the unique education, experience, and actions of its people, but his historical conception of American identity also fused with older religious strands in American thought to suggest that the new nation's triumphs must also have expressed the will of God. Momentous events did not occur simply by chance, in Bancroft's view, so he wanted Americans to see the purposeful direction of their own history in his books—which sought "to follow the steps by which a favoring Providence, calling our institutions into being, has conducted the country to its present happiness and glory." Belief in the divine guidance of history was of course a prominent theme in the New England Puritanism that had fostered much of the popular confidence in the justice of America's revolutionary cause. As Bancroft described it, however, this American religious tradition was also a key source of the national belief in personal freedom, because Protestantism encouraged the "right of private judgment." Drawing inspiration and confidence from this faith, Americans avoided the skepticism that afflicted Europeans and found a sensible religious justification for their passionate belief in civic freedom. Calvinist churches helped prevent the political excesses that accompanied the outbreak of revolutions in Europe, Bancroft argued, but the divine spirit in America spread far beyond the churches to give spiritual meaning to the whole society. "The spirit of God breathes through the combined intelligence of the people," Bancroft wrote in one of his enthusiastic summaries of America's distinctive national achievements. There had inevitably been much British resistance to America's revolutionary movement in the 1770s, and yet all the power of Britain's army and navy failed to stop a "change which Divine Wisdom ordained, and which no human policy or force could hold back."[28]

Although God supported the national mission, America needed revolutionary soldiers and militiamen to carry the divine will into historical reality. Bancroft therefore invoked familiar religious images as he described American soldiers and casualties in stories that resembled older narratives about holy martyrs and the deaths of good Christians. The first militiamen to die at Lexington in 1775, for example, "gave their lives in testimony to the rights of mankind," thus demonstrating their steadfast allegiance to the most enduring principles of human history. Their deaths had been a tragedy for their grieving families, but the nation would always remember these "lowly men who proved themselves worthy of their forerunners, and whose children rise up and call them blessed."[29] Death led to immortality for these militiamen, because a thankful nation would never forget how their sacrifices had given freedom to America. The dead "Minutemen" of Lexington continued to inspire their children and every subsequent defender of American independence, just as they had drawn courage from the ideals and actions of *their* ancestors. The continuity of the nation, in other words, appeared in the deaths as well as the lives of its most honored heroes.

Soldiers who rallied to their nation's defense, however, were protecting more than the ideals of political freedom or national sovereignty, because the intrusion of British soldiers was also a physical assault on the families, livelihood, and homes of the American people. When messengers warned the scattered population of Massachusetts about the advancing British troops in 1775, the "children trembled as they were scared out of their sleep" and the "wives with heaving breasts bravely seconded their husbands" as the men marched off to face the enemy. Using the typical nationalist rhetoric of family honor, Bancroft portrayed the fears in Massachusetts to stress the decisive public and personal issues that came together in the American struggle against hostile British troops. "Come forth, champions of liberty," Bancroft wrote in one of his lyrical passages; "now free your country; protect your sons and daughters, your wives and homesteads; rescue the houses of the God of your fathers, the franchises handed down from your ancestors. Now all is at stake; the battle is for all."[30] This first day of battle at Lexington and Concord would be followed by long, difficult years of warfare, but from the beginning there was no historical role and no honor for those weak men who wanted to hide or compromise or abandon their families to the fury of hostile soldiers. As Bancroft told the story, everyone had to choose sides, and there was no doubt about which side was right.

Most Americans saw the justice of the revolutionary cause, Bancroft reported, so they rallied to the new American army and the patriot cause with exemplary unity and commitment. To be sure, some people in every region of the country remained loyal to the British king, yet Americans from South Carolina to New Hampshire joined together in a shared revolutionary commitment to the national ideals of freedom and self-government. This remarkable (retrospective) eighteenth-century national unity carried obvious contemporary implications for Bancroft, because America was falling into bitter sectional conflicts while he was writing his history of revolutionary events. The danger of such conflicts pushed Bancroft toward a growing emphasis on a once-existing national unity that had disappeared in the middle of the nineteenth century. When Bancroft discussed the political conflicts in prerevolutionary Boston, for example, he gave detailed attention to the unified support that came to Bostonians from people in the Carolinas and Virginia. All good patriots in the North *and* the South had rallied to the same cause and supported the same American principles. "But the love of liberty in America did not flash like electricity on the surface," Bancroft explained in 1858; "it penetrated the mass with magnetic energy.... [And] the continent, as 'one great commonwealth,' made the cause of Boston its own."[31] Here then was the historical model for later generations, if only they would recognize the national ideals they shared instead of harping on how they differed and disagreed. The history of America was for Bancroft a history of growing national unity, which developed out of a common belief in the nation's enduring political creed. Yet the bonds that connected the white population also excluded other races, so the unity of the political ideals was undermined by the disunity and conflicts of racial difference.

Bancroft assumed that deep differences of history, culture, and race separated African Americans from the "Anglo-Saxons" who constituted the vital core of American national life, much as he assumed that racial and cultural differences separated Native Americans from European Americans (see chapter 5). Whereas the European Americans arrived in the New World with a strong cultural legacy, religious traditions, and a dynamic language, the Africans were brought to America with none of the essential tools of civilization. In fact, Bancroft argued in one of his early volumes, "they came with the limited faculties of uncivilized man," which meant they had "no common language, no abiding usages, no worship, no nationality." Such people could thus learn about civilization only through the skills and language of their "masters," Bancroft explained, and despite all the "horrors of slavery and the slave trade, the masters had, in part at least, performed the office of advancing and civilizing the Negro."[32]

The weakness of both the Native American and African civilizations, as Bancroft described them, placed the destiny of America in the hands of the "Anglo-Saxon" race, whose institutions and language quickly came to dominate the continent and to give America its distinctive national identity. Once the French had been driven from their bases of North American power in the 1760s, the whole continent lay open to "the Teutonic race, with its strong tendency to individuality and freedom" and with its distinctive English language. "Go forth, then, language of Milton and Hampden, language of my country," Bancroft wrote in his concluding summary of The Seven Years War, "take possession of the North American Continent! . . . Utter boldly and spread widely . . . the thoughts of the coming apostles of the people's liberty."[33] English became the language of American culture, freedom, and expansion; and, as Bancroft reminded his readers, English remained the enduring language of American union.

Bancroft was a strong Unionist during the American Civil War, and (despite some criticisms of abolitionists) he definitely wanted slavery to disappear—in part because he thought it was an immoral institution and in part because he saw slavery as a major obstacle to the national unity he cherished. At the end of the Civil War he aligned himself with President Andrew Johnson in opposition to the radical Reconstructionists and gave Johnson advice as he prepared his first presidential speech to Congress. Even more significant for a staunch advocate of national union, Bancroft delivered the official memorial oration on Lincoln's life in the United States Congress on February 12, 1866, using the occasion to show how Lincoln had expressed the highest ideals of the American people.[34] Yet Bancroft's conception of America remained closely connected to the Jacksonian nationalism of the 1830s or 1840s, which may partly explain why the most influential statement of America's national ideology in the 1860s came from Abraham Lincoln himself rather than from his Congressional eulogist. No historian or political leader would duplicate Bancroft's ten-volume account of the American past, but Lincoln managed to turn Bancroft's historical narrative into a vision for the future with 267 words that summarized the self-defined meaning of America more memorably than all the volumes that Bancroft (or other historians) ever produced.

The Gettysburg Address and American National Identity

Authors such as Philip Freneau and George Bancroft made significant contributions to the ongoing description of America that enabled people to "imagine" their national identity and territory. Although the American narratives differed from many of the nationalist narratives in Europe, they also developed common nationalist claims for the political, historical, and cultural uniqueness of their own national society. American writers filled their texts with typical nationalist allusions to religion, literature, military heroes, and virtuous families—and even the allegedly "Eastern" European themes of race and language could be found in American discussions of Indians, African Americans, or immigrants. Yet the writings of American poets and historians did not become part of the "sacred canon" of national texts that included the Declaration of Independence, the Constitution, the Bill of Rights, and (after the 1860s) Abraham Lincoln's Gettysburg Address. The famous, short speech that Lincoln delivered in November 1863 at the site of the greatest battle of America's Civil War quickly became one of the defining texts of American national identity, and as such, an excellent canonical example of the recurring emotional themes that have given nationalism its power in the public and personal lives of modern people.

Lincoln's speech at the commemoration of the dead at Gettysburg lasted about two minutes and consisted of the following three paragraphs:

> Four score and seven years ago our fathers brought forth on this continent, a new nation, conceived in Liberty, and dedicated to the proposition that all men are created equal.
>
> Now we are engaged in a great civil war, testing whether that nation, or any nation so conceived and so dedicated, can long endure. We are met on a great battle-field of that war. We have come to dedicate a portion of that field, as a final resting place for those who gave their lives that that nation might live. It is altogether fitting and proper that we should do this.
>
> But, in a larger sense, we can not dedicate—we can not consecrate—we can not hallow—this ground. The brave men, living and dead, who struggled here, have consecrated it, far above our poor power to add or detract. The world will little note, nor long remember what we say here, but it can never forget what they did here. It is for us the living, rather, to be dedicated here to the unfinished work which they who fought here have thus far so nobly advanced. It is rather for us to be here dedicated to the great task remaining before us—that from these honored dead we take increased devotion to that cause for which they gave the last full measure of devotion—that we here highly resolve that these dead shall not have died in vain—that this nation, un-

der God, shall have a new birth of freedom—and that government of the people, by the people, for the people, shall not perish from the earth.[35]

Contemporaries immediately recognized Lincoln's brief speech as a dramatic summary of the American national creed. George Bancroft asked for and received from Lincoln a copy for a volume on "American authors" he published in 1864, and later generations would recite these words at countless celebrations of America's distinctive national history.

When one places the address in the more general context of modern nationalism, however, it becomes a remarkably succinct account of the life-and-death themes that have inspired emotional allegiance to every successful nationalist movement or nation-state. Delivered on a battlefield (always a privileged, "hallowed" ground for nationalists), it began with references to both the national "fathers" and the central political claim of the national identity—"that all men are created equal." The dramatic, historical significance of that claim then emerged in the following paragraph, which stressed that (1) the national legacy was facing its greatest challenge, and (2) the living generation must honor "those who here gave their lives that that nation might live." Lincoln's phrase thus evoked the ancient, Christlike image of sacrifice that has long given powerful religious force to the nationalist reverence for dead soldiers.

The ultimate lesson of this sacrifice, though, went beyond the memory of the dead to the essential message of the final paragraph, in which Lincoln urged his compatriots to recommit themselves to new action and new sacrifices in the future. The long struggle was not yet over; indeed, it required an "increased devotion" to make sure that the dead "shall not have died in vain." This new, resolute devotion to the cause of the national "fathers" and the deceased soldiers would inevitably be difficult, but such commitments would give new meaning to both the sacrifice of the dead and the future work of the living. In the end, "this nation, under God," could achieve the ultimate triumph of its national mission through a "new birth of freedom," thereby bringing new life out of painful deaths and a new historical message to the whole world. The victory of the national, unionist cause, in short, would prove "that government of the people, by the people, for the people, shall not perish from the earth."

Lincoln's speech therefore became a canonical nationalist text because it offered a brief, moving homage to the nation's dead and a brief, inspiring vision of the nation's future mission and unity. It would appeal to later generations as a compelling summary of the most general national ideas, as an exemplary recognition of virtuous soldiers, and as a reminder of the national dangers that must always be opposed. Lincoln never mentioned specific enemies (e.g., Confederate generals or evil slaveholders), but he issued strong warnings about the dangers of insufficient commitment to the national cause or insufficient honor to the sacrifices of the dead. These broad themes gave Lincoln's address a distinguished place in the endless nationalist campaign to link the living to the dead, celebrate the universal meaning of the nation's distinctive historical destiny, and promote new actions to ensure the nation's future virtue and influence. More generally, the Gettysburg Address suggests why the nationalisms and nationalist identities that have generated and sustained so much of the modern world's violence and warfare have also generated and sustained some of the modern world's most valuable aspirations for freedom and human rights.

Conclusion:
Nationalism in the Modern World

The history of nationalism continues of course far beyond the eighteenth- and nineteenth-century revolutions, wars, writers, and nationalist movements of Europe and North America. Although it would be impossible to write (or read) a complete, global history of nationalism's vast influence throughout the modern world, the historical analysis of nationalist ideologies and conflicts since the nineteenth century could lead into virtually every sphere of politics, economics, culture, diplomacy, warfare, religion, and education. More specifically, a comprehensive account of nationalism's evolving ideas and cultural power would have to describe the expansion of Western imperialisms after 1880 and the military arms race that led to the Great War of 1914–1918. The violence, propaganda, and memory of World War I could provide excellent examples of how nationalism has served to mobilize the populations of modern nation-states; and that war's enduring legacy (which included the Russian Revolution, the rise of Fascism, and the creation of new national governments in central Europe) could be traced through most of the later national events of twentieth-century history, including World War II and the Cold War.

The wider political and cultural significance of nationalism could never be understood, however, without detailed analysis of the worldwide, anticolonial movements that developed rapidly in the decades after World War II. Historians and political theorists argue about the cultural characteristics of these movements and about their relation to other political traditions such as socialism or liberalism, and yet familiar nationalist themes clearly emerged in every popular, successful independence movement—from India to China, from Algeria to Vietnam, from Mozambique to Indonesia. Redefining and extending the anti-imperial arguments that eighteenth-century Americans had used to justify their revolutionary war against Britain, new anticolonial campaigns destroyed the empires of Western governments and created new national states in Asia, Africa, and the Middle East.

The comprehensive history of modern nationalism could not end with the establishment of new national states, however, because it would have to continue into the conflicts of Israel and the Palestinians, Bosnia and Serbia, India and Pakistan, Vietnam and Cambodia, or America and Iraq, to name only a few of the late-twentieth-century sites of nationalist violence. Meanwhile, the analyst of nationalism's ubiquitous, contemporary consequences would need to consider the bloodshed in Northern Ireland, the terrorism of Basque separatists in Spain, the political and linguistic demands of the Quebecois in Canada, the internal and external responses to the reunification of Germany, the flags and national anthems at the Olympic Games, or the anger over French tests of nuclear weapons in the South Pacific. And there would be even more important historical evidence for a would-be student of nationalism to investigate in the resurgence of fundamentalist, religious nationalisms or in the debates about immigration, education, language usage, and multiculturalism that provoke strong emotions in every region of the world.

These few examples barely begin to indicate the extraordinary historical impact of nationalist ideas, institutions, rituals, and political movements, but they suggest why nationalism may well have become the most pervasive, influential "ism" of the modern era. Like all important "isms," nationalism has often taken significantly different forms in the many places, cultures, institutions, and conflicts in which it has appeared, and the emotional identification with nationalist causes has varied as people have lived through periods of war or peace or social conflicts. Yet there are also patterns of thought and action that reappear in almost every nationalism and give this "ism" certain continuities across the centuries and cultures of modern history. Although this book has dealt solely with examples of nationalist action and writings in Europe and the United States during the decisive, formative era between the 1770s and 1860s, similar themes can be found in all the nationalist movements and writings of other continents and other times.

All nationalisms have depended on narratives about the distinctive historical, cultural, and political traits that make one's own nation different from other nations or societies. These narratives of national difference create the boundaries of national space, time, and culture within which people are able to define their national identities. Definitions of identity and difference thus recur in all the more specific nationalist conceptions of political and cultural independence. Repeating the earlier claims of American and French revolutionaries, nationalists have always believed in the existence of a sovereign "people," whose will should be embodied in government institutions. Democratic and authoritarian political movements alike have typically defined their ideas as the authentic political voice of the people or the true nation, and they have used the language of human rights to justify their demands for national independence and autonomy.

The sovereign national state has therefore become the essential protection for the sovereignty of the people, but this political definition of the distinctive national will has usually merged with other definitions of a distinctive national culture. All nationalisms have needed intellectuals who describe the meaning of the national history, language, literature, and art, and who also work to communicate this national narrative through schools, newspapers, and books. The story of national events, leaders, and traditions must always be retold, much as Michelet told the story of France or Bancroft told the story of America; and twentieth-century nationalists found effective, new ways to narrate the national culture in films, radio, and television.

The stories of nations have often gained the greatest emotional power when they merged with traditional religious ideas about moral duties or reverence for the dead. Nationalists in Europe and North America borrowed from Judaism and Christianity to develop their descriptions of Chosen Peoples and messianic missions, but other nationalisms have been equally successful in drawing on Islam, Hinduism, Shintoism, or other religious traditions to give transcendent meanings to a national cause. Nationalisms have thus resembled the world's most enduring religions in explaining the essence of individual lives (a national soul), in creating a social community (the national "family" that supports and asks sacrifices from everyone), and in providing consolation for death (the nation is eternal). Nationalisms have become closely connected to the deepest human anxieties about life and death, in part because they promise a kind of immortality for the dead, and in part because they promise a better life for the nation's children and future generations. Most nationalists have taken a deep interest in the continuing reproduction of the nation and celebrated the national significance of "good families," "good mothers," and "good fathers." These biological preoccupations have also led to racial nationalisms in Africa and Asia that can be compared to theories about race or ethnicity in Europe and America, but even nationalists who ignore race tend to worry about the purity of families and the dangers of "abnormal" sex. A healthy, well-ordered domestic life becomes linked to a healthy, well-ordered public life in most nationalist definitions of virtuous national identities.

This linkage between the life (or reproduction) of the nation and the life (or death) of the individual gives nationalism much of its exceptional emotional power. Cultural identities and personal identities fuse in nationalist definitions of groups and individuals, which may help to explain why so many modern people have been willing to kill or die in the name of their national states or cultures. Narratives of national identity connect the individual to a social community and offer at least partial satisfaction to deep human desires for status, immortality, power, freedom, and security. These desires draw strength from both the conscious and unconscious processes of individual psychology and cultural tradition, and they have by no means disappeared from our constantly changing history of political conflict, economic production, and technological innovation. Although the various cultures of the world have become steadily more connected through trade, travel, education, and communications, the identity-shaping definitions of cultural and historical difference remain crucial for individuals, social groups, and national governments in every modern society. Nationalism may well take new forms or evolve differently in the future, but the deep, overlapping structures of personal and cultural identity give us good reasons to assume that emotionally charged, nationalist identities, ideas, and conflicts will continue to be powerful historical forces in the lives of most people during the century that lies ahead.

Chronology

1690   John Locke publishes *Two Treatises of Government;* claims that government derives from "contract" with people.

1762   Jean-Jacques Rousseau publishes *The Social Contract;* argues for a government that expresses "general will."

1776   American Declaration of Independence from Britain.

1776–1783   American Revolutionary War.

1784   J. G. Herder publishes *Reflections on the Philosophy of the History of Mankind;* stresses unique cultures.

1789   United States of America created through new national Constitution.

1789   Abbé Sieyès publishes "What Is the Third Estate?" and claims that common people are the true "nation."

1789   French Revolution begins with Declaration of "The Rights of Man and Citizen."

1790   Edmund Burke publishes *Reflections on the Revolution in France;* describes Britain's unique national history.

1791   France enters revolutionary wars against European kings.

1792   C. J. Rouget de Lisle writes "The Marsaillaise" in France.

1792   France declares itself a sovereign Republic.

1799–1815   Napoleon holds power in France and wages wars in Europe; opposition to Napoleon fosters nationalism.

1806–1825   Latin American political movements declare independence from Spain and establish new national governments.

1808   J. G. Fichte publishes *Addresses to the German Nation,* calling for defense of German national spirit.

1812   Jacob and Wilhelm Grimm publish *Grimm's Fairy Tales* in Germany.

1813   Ernst Moritz Arndt publishes *The Spirit of the Times,* Part III, describing German national soul and military struggle.

1814   Francis Scott Key writes "The Star-Spangled Banner" in the United States.

1823   United States issues Monroe Doctrine, opposing European interventions to reestablish colonies in America.

1830–1831   Revolution in France inspires new nationalist movements in Italy and Poland.

1833   Leopold von Ranke publishes essay, "The Great Powers," stressing the political rivalries of national states.

1834   George Bancroft begins publishing *History of the United States.*

1837   Ralph Waldo Emerson publishes "The American Scholar."

1840–1844   Adam Mickiewicz lectures on Slavic culture and literature at the Collège de France in Paris.

1844   Joseph Mazzini begins publishing essays on Italian culture that will later appear in *The Duties of Man.*

1845   The phrase "Manifest Destiny" is first used in the United States to justify American expansion to the West.

1846	Jules Michelet publishes his book on France's national character, *The People*.
1847–1853	Jules Michelet publishes seven-volume *History of the French Revolution*.
1848	Nationalist movements support revolutions in France, Germany, and central Europe.
1848	Jacob Grimm publishes his *History of the German Language*.
1853–1855	Arthur de Gobineau publishes *Essay on the Inequality of the Races*.
1859–1870	Unification of Italy.
1861–1865	Civil War in the United States.
1863	Abraham Lincoln gives the Gettysburg Address.
1866–1871	Unification of Germany.
1870–1871	Franco-Prussian War.
1880–1914	Expansion of Imperialism; imperialist rivalries between Britain, France, Germany, United States, and Spain.
1882	Ernest Renan publishes "What Is a Nation?"
1904–1905	Russo-Japanese War shows Japan's national power.
1911	Chinese National Revolution overthrows Manchu Imperial Dynasty
1914–1918	World War I.
1917	Beginning of the Russian Revolution.
1919	Versailles Peace Conference affirms National Self-Determination, but extends British and French Empires.
1922	Fascists seize power in Italy.
1933	Nazi seizure of power in Germany.
1939–1945	World War II.
1945	Creation of the United Nations.
1946–1954	Vietnamese war for independence from France.
1947	India and Pakistan gain independence from Britain.

1948   First Arab-Israeli War in the Middle East.

1949   Chinese Revolution leads to establishment of the People's Republic of China.

1956–1962   Independence movements replace British and French colonies with new national governments in Africa.

1961   Frantz Fanon publishes *The Wretched of the Earth;* describes anger of colonized people fighting for national independence in Algeria.

1964–1975   Vietnam War between Vietnamese communists and the United States; ends with unification of Vietnam under communist government.

1967   Arab-Israeli War in the Middle East.

1982–1998   Continuing conflicts between Israel and Palestinians.

1991   Persian Gulf War; American-led forces expel Iraqi army from Kuwait.

1991   Breakup of Soviet Union into various national states.

1991–1996   Breakup of Yugoslavia and continuing war over Serb conquests in Bosnia.

Notes and References

CHAPTER 1

1. Nathan Hale's last words appear in Henry Phelps Johnston, *Nathan Hale 1776: Biography and Memorials* (New Haven, 1914), p. 129; quoted passages of "The Marsaillaise" are from the translation in *The New Encyclopaedia Britannica*, 15th ed., vol. 7 (Chicago, 1993), p. 875; Johann Gottlieb Fichte, *Addresses to the German Nation*, trans. R. F. Jones and G. H. Turnbull (Chicago, 1922), p. 253.

2. Hans Kohn, *The Idea of Nationalism: A Study in its Origins and Background* (New York, 1944), p. 10.

3. Liah Greenfeld, *Nationalism: Five Roads to Modernity* (Cambridge, Mass., 1992), p. 21; her account of early nationalist ideas in England and France appears in ibid., pp. 29–188. For other views of the relation between nationalism and modernity, see Anthony D. Smith, *Theories of Nationalism*, 2d ed. (New York, 1983) and Ernest Gellner, *Nations and Nationalism* (Ithaca, 1983).

4. Anthony D. Smith, "The Nation: Invented, Imagined, Reconstructed?" in *Reimagining the Nation*, ed. Marjorie Ringrose and Adam J. Lerner (Buckingham and Philadelphia, 1993), pp. 15–16. Smith develops similar themes in several books, including *The Ethnic Origins of Nations* (Oxford, 1986) and *National Identity* (London, 1991).

5. Gellner, *Nations and Nationalism*, pp. 35–39, 138–142; quotations on pp. 35, 39. Eric Hobsbawm also emphasizes the connections between

nationalism and modernizing economies in *Nations and Nationalisms Since 1780: Programme, Myth, Reality* (Cambridge, 1990), pp. 9–10, 24–31.

   6. David M. Potter, "The Historian's Use of Nationalism and Vice Versa," *American Historical Review* 67 (1962): 932.

   7. Peter Alter, *Nationalism*, 2d ed. (London, 1994), p. 4.

   8. Greenfeld, *Nationalism*, pp. 15–16.

   9. Ibid., p. 490.

   10. Stuart Hall, "Cultural Identity and Diaspora," in *Colonial Discourse and Post-Colonial Theory: A Reader*, ed. Patrick Williams and Laura Chrisman (New York, 1993), pp. 394–95, 401–2.

   11. For examples of the evolving theoretical emphasis on the role of language in historical experience and understanding, see Dominick LaCapra and Steven L. Kaplan, eds., *Modern European Intellectual History: Reappraisals and New Perspectives* (Ithaca, 1982); Lynn Hunt, ed., *The New Cultural History* (Berkeley, 1989); and Frank Ankersmit and Hans Kellner, eds., *A New Philosophy of History* (London, 1995).

   12. Benedict Anderson, *Imagined Communities: Reflections on the Origin and Spread of Nationalism*, rev. ed. (London, 1991), pp. 6–7.

   13. Eric Hobsbawm and Terence Ranger, eds., *The Invention of Tradition* (Cambridge, 1983).

   14. Eric Hobsbawm, "Introduction: Inventing Traditions," in ibid., pp. 2, 13–14.

   15. Homi K. Bhabha, "DissemiNation: Time, Narrative, and the Margins of the Modern Nation," in Homi K. Bhabha, ed., *Nation and Narration* (London, 1990), pp. 297, 299–300.

   16. Peter Sahlins, *Boundaries: The Making of France and Spain in the Pyrenees* (Berkeley and Los Angeles, 1989), p. 270.

   17. Greenfeld, *Nationalism*, pp. 11–12. For examples of the distinctions that have long been used to differentiate nationalisms, see Peter Alter, *Nationalism*, pp. 19–20, 26–27; Hans Kohn, *Prelude to Nation-States: The French and German Experience, 1789–1815* (Princeton, 1967); Louis Dumont, *German Ideology: From France to Germany and Back* (Chicago, 1994); Rogers Brubaker, *Citizenship and Nationhood in France and Germany* (Cambridge, Mass., 1992); Friedrich Meinecke, *Cosmopolitanism and the National State*, trans. Robert B. Kimer (Princeton, 1970), and John Plamenatz, "Two Types of Nationalism," in *Nationalism: The Nature and Evolution of an Idea*, ed. Eugene Kamenka (New York, 1976), pp. 22–36.

   18. See, for example, the account of derivative nationalisms in Plamenatz, "Two Types of Nationalism," pp. 29–34, and the critique of this view in Partha Chatterjee, *Nationalist Thought and the Colonial World: A Derivative Discourse?* (London, 1986), pp. 1–30.

   19. The classic account of how these rapidly spreading political ideas transformed Western political cultures appears in the synthetic

work of R. R. Palmer, *The Age of the Democratic Revolution: A Political History of Europe and America, 1760–1800,* 2 vols. (Princeton, 1959, 1964). More recent studies of these revolutionary changes include Lynn Hunt, *Politics, Culture, and Class in the French Revolution* (Berkeley, 1984), and Gordon S. Wood, *The Radicalism of the American Revolution: How a Revolution Transformed a Monarchical Society into a Democratic One Unlike Any That Had Ever Existed* (New York, 1991).

CHAPTER 2

1. On the development of nationalist themes among social elites in early modern England and France, see Greenfeld, *Nationalism,* pp. 44–70, 145–72. For concise accounts of how the "nation" was redefined during the French Revolution, see Brian Jenkins, *Nationalism in France: Class and Nation since 1789* (London, 1990), pp. 11–22, and Otto Dann's "Introduction," in *Nationalism in the Age of the French Revolution,* ed. Otto Dann and John Dinwiddy (London, 1988), pp. 5–10.

2. Kohn, *Idea of Nationalism,* p. 237.

3. Jean-Jacques Rousseau, *On the Social Contract,* trans. Donald A. Cress, intro. Peter Gay (Indianapolis, 1987), pp. 24, 29. On the subsequent history of the links between nationalisms and modern states, see John Breuilly, *Nationalism and the State,* 2d ed. (Manchester, 1993).

4. Dumont, *German Ideology,* pp. 7–8.

5. Rousseau, *Social Contract,* pp. 26, 34.

6. Kohn, *Idea of Nationalism,* p. 226.

7. For more on the role of nationalism in the social transition to nineteenth-century liberal societies, see Hobsbawm, *Nations and Nationalism,* pp. 38–43.

8. Anderson, *Imagined Communities,* p. 191.

9. Thomas Jefferson, "The Declaration of Independence, As Amended by the Committee and by Congress," in *The Papers of Thomas Jefferson,* vol. 1, ed. Julian P. Boyd et al. (Princeton, 1950), pp. 429, 432.

10. Thomas Paine, "Common Sense," in Paine, *Collected Writings,* ed. Eric Foner (New York, 1995), pp. 5–6, 36.

11. David Ramsay, "An Oration on the Advantages of American Independence," in *David Ramsay, 1749–1815: Selections from His Writings* [Transactions of the American Philosophical Society, vol. 55, pt. 4], ed. Robert L. Brunhouse (Philadelphia, 1965), pp. 188, 190.

12. Philip Freneau, "POEM on . . . gallant capt. Paul Jones," in *The Newspaper Verse of Philip Freneau,* ed. Judith R. Hiltner (Troy, N.Y., 1986), pp. 80–81.

13. Philip Freneau, "[The Popularity of the French Cause]," *National Gazette,* 22 May 1793, in *The Prose of Philip Freneau,* ed. Philip M.

Marsh (New Brunswick, N.J., 1955), p. 299. For examples of Freneau's poetic commentary on the French American connections, see "On the Fourteenth of July," in Hiltner, ed., *Newspaper Verse*, pp. 498–99.

14. Thomas Paine, *Rights of Man*, in Paine, *Collected Writings*, pp. 549, 555–56.

15. The priest was Augustin Barruel, who denounced "*nationalisme*" in his book *Mémoires pour servir à l'histoire du Jacobinisme* (1798). For more on the development of the word, see Eugene Kamenka, "Political Nationalism—the Evolution of the Idea," in Kamenka, ed., *Nationalism*, pp. 8–9.

16. Greenfeld, *Nationalism*, pp. 91–188; see also David A. Bell, "Lingua Populi, Lingua Dei: Language, Religion, and the Origins of French Revolutionary Nationalism," *American Historical Review* 100 (1995):1403–37.

17. Hunt, *Politics, Culture, and Class*, pp. 213–36, quotation on p. 214.

18. "Declaration of the Rights of Man and Citizen," in *The French Revolution and Human Rights: A Brief Documentary History*, ed. and trans. Lynn Hunt (New York, 1996), p. 78.

19. Abbé Sieyès, "What Is the Third Estate?" in ibid., pp. 67–69.

20. "Instruction Concerning the Era of the Republic and the Division of the Year, Decreed by the National Convention," in *A Documentary Survey of the French Revolution*, ed. John Hall Stewart (New York, 1951), p. 513.

21. "Statement of French Foreign Policy," (14 April 1792) and "Circular from the Paris Jacobins to Local Branches of the Club" (5 April 1793), in ibid., pp. 285, 287, 428.

22. "Chant du départ," quoted in John A. Lynn, *The Bayonets of the Republic: Motivation and Tactics in the Army of Revolutionary France, 1791–94* (Urbana, Ill., 1984), p. 148.

23. "Decree Establishing the Levy *en masse*," in Stewart, ed., *Documentary Survey of French Revolution*, p. 473.

24. Rousseau, *Social Contract*, pp. 96–102; Hunt, *Politics, Culture, and Class*, pp. 19–119; and Maurice Agulhon, *Marianne into Battle: Republican Imagery and Symbolism in France, 1789–1880*, trans. Janet Lloyd (Cambridge, 1981), pp. 30–36.

25. S. Sherlock, *Opinion sur la nécessité de rendre l'instruction publique commune à tous les enfants des Français* (Year VII [1799]), quoted in Mona Ozouf, *Festivals and the French Revolution*, trans. Alan Sheridan (Cambridge, Mass., 1988), p. 200.

26. François de Neufchâteau, "Hymn to Liberty," quoted in Emmet Kennedy, *A Cultural History of the French Revolution* (New Haven, 1989), p. 281.

27. On this Bonapartist transition, see Jenkins, *Nationalism in France,* pp. 31–42, and Jacques Godechot, "The New Concept of the Nation and its Diffusion in Europe," in Dann and Dinwiddy, eds., *Nationalism in Age of French Revolution,* pp. 23–26.

28. For discussion of both the British mobilization and its possible effects on the nation's political culture, see Linda Colley, *Britons: Forging the Nation 1707–1837* (New Haven, 1992), pp. 283–319, 371–72; quotation on p. 303.

29. Edmund Burke, *Reflections on the Revolution in France,* ed. J. G. A. Pocock (Indianapolis, 1987), pp. 27–28, 75–76. On the more general conservatism of English national responses to the French Revolution, see John Dinwiddy, "England," in Dann and Dinwiddy, eds., *Nationalism in Age of French Revolution,* pp. 53–70.

30. Friedrich von Gentz to Christian Garve, 5 December 1790, quoted in Hans Kohn, *Prelude to Nation-States: The French and German Experience, 1789–1815* (Princeton, 1967), pp. 133–34.

31. Franz Dumont, "The Rhineland," in Dann and Dinwiddy, eds., *Nationalism in Age of French Revolution,* pp. 157–170.

32. On the admiration for France and liberal forms of nationalism in Germany, see Hans Kohn, *The Mind of Germany: The Education of a Nation* (New York, 1960), pp. 22–48, and Kohn, *Prelude to Nation-States,* pp. 144–157; Dumont, *German Ideology,* pp. 90–134; and Peter Alter, "Nationalism and Liberalism in Modern German History," in *Nationality, Patriotism, and Nationalism in Liberal Democratic Societies,* ed. Roger Michener (St. Paul, Minn., 1993), pp. 81–87.

33. Friedrich von Gentz, *The French and American Revolutions Compared,* trans. John Quincy Adams, in Stefan T. Possony, *Three Revolutions* (Chicago, 1959), pp. 67, 86.

34. Fichte, *Addresses,* pp. 249, 254.

35. Ernst Moritz Arndt, *Geist der Zeit,* Part 3 (1814), quoted in Hagen Schulze, *The Course of German Nationalism: From Frederick the Great to Bismarck, 1763–1867,* trans. Sarah Hansbury-Tension (Cambridge, 1991) p. 50; Joseph Görres, in the *Rheinischer Merkur* (May 11, 1815), quoted in Kohn, *Prelude to Nation-States,* p. 293.

CHAPTER 3

1. Johann Gottfried von Herder, *Reflections on the Philosophy of the History of Mankind,* trans. T. O. Churchill, abridged and introduced by Frank E. Manuel (Chicago, 1968), p. 7; emphasis added. Fichte, *Addresses,* p. 215.

2. H. H. Cludius, excerpt from *Musterpredigten über alle Evangelien und Episteln des Jahres, so wie über freie Texte und Casualfälle . . . ,* vol. IX

(1819), p. 327, quoted in Arlie J. Hoover, *The Gospel of Nationalism: German Patriotic Preaching from Napoleon to Versailles* (Stuttgart, 1986), p. 60.

3. Fichte, *Addresses*, pp. 223–24.

4. For an introduction to the communicative acts that link politics to language, see Michael Townson, *Mother-Tongue and Fatherland: Language and Politics in German* (Manchester, 1992), pp. 6–33. For examples of the cultural diffusion of nationalist ideas, see George L. Mosse, *The Nationalization of the Masses: Political Symbolism and Mass Movements in Germany from the Napoleonic Wars through the Third Reich* (New York, 1975).

5. Grégoire's report to the National Convention appears in Michel de Certeau, Dominque Julia, and Jacques Revel, *Une politique de la langue: la Révolution française et les patois* (Paris, 1975), pp. 300–317.

6. Johann Georg Breidenstein, *Predigt an Dank- und Befreiungsfeste zu Homburg vor der Hohe den achten Mai 1814* (1814), quoted in Hoover, *Gospel of Nationalism*, p. 60. Fichte, *Addresses*, p. 83.

7. Adam Mickiewicz, *Les Slaves: Cours professé au Collège de France (1842–1844)* (Paris, 1914), pp. 323–24. On the problem of creating pure national cultures, see Homi Bhabha's introduction and concluding essay ("DissemiNation: Time, Narrative, and the Margins of the Modern Nation") in Bhabha, ed., *Nation and Narration*, pp. 1–7, 291–322.

8. Grégoire, "Sur la nécessité et les moyens d'anéantir les patois . . . ," in de Certeau, Julia, and Revel, *Une politique de la langue*, p. 303.

9. Bertrand Barère, "Rapport du Comité de Salut Public sur les idiomes," in ibid., p. 295. On the linguistic debates and policies of the French Revolution (with comparisons to religious missions in earlier eras), see Bell, "Lingua Populi," pp. 1403–37.

10. Fichte, *Addresses*, p. 15.

11. Joseph Mazzini, *The Duties of Man and Other Essays*, (London, 1907), p. 87.

12. On the general diffusion of nationalist ideas and languages in education, see Gellner, *Nations and Nationalism*, pp. 19–62; for examples of education policies in specific national contexts, see R. R. Palmer, *The Improvement of Humanity: Education and the French Revolution* (Princeton, 1985) [data on government expenditures, pp. 334–335]; and (for a later period) Eric Hobsbawm, "Mass-Producing Traditions: Europe, 1870–1914," in Hobsbawm and Ranger, eds., *Invention of Tradition*, pp. 263–307.

13. Anderson, *Imagined Communities*, p. 46. On the role of communications in nationalism, see Karl W. Deutsch, *Nationalism and Social Communication: An Inquiry into the Foundations of Nationality* (New York, 1953), pp. 71–78.

14. Fichte, *Addresses*, p. 217.

15. Ralph Waldo Emerson, "The American Scholar," in Emerson, *Selected Essays*, ed. Larzer Ziff (New York, 1982), pp. 103–105.

16. For examples of such arguments, see Elie Kedourie, *Nationalism,* 4th ed. (Oxford, 1993), pp. 33–43, and Greenfeld, *Nationalism,* pp. 293–352.

17. Anderson, *Imagined Communities,* pp. 24–36. On the importance of novels in the shaping of national identities, see also the essays by Timothy Brennan ("The National Longing for Form") and Doris Sommer ("Irresistible Romance: the Foundational Fictions of Latin America") in Bhabha, ed., *Nation and Narration,* pp. 44–98.

18. On the political significance of Jacob Grimm and other German philologists, see Townson, *Mother-Tongue and Fatherland,* pp. 80–110.

19. Fichte, *Addresses,* pp. 78–79, 126.

20. Mickiewicz, *Les Slaves,* pp. 4, 12, 21–23.

21. Emerson, "The Poet," in Emerson, *Selected Essays,* pp. 261, 263, 271, 281.

22. Ernest Renan, "What Is a Nation?" [1882] trans. Martin Thom, in Bhabha, ed., *Nation and Narration,* p. 11.

23. Ibid., p. 19.

24. For an introduction to this era's contribution to a new historical mindedness, see Stephen Bann, *Romanticism and the Rise of History* (New York, 1995), pp. 3–29.

25. Fichte, *Addresses,* p. 264.

26. Leopold von Ranke, "On the Relation of and Distinction between History and Politics," [1836] in Ranke, *The Secret of World History: Selected Writings on the Art and Science of History,* ed. and trans. Roger Wines (New York, 1981), pp. 110, 112.

27. Leopold von Ranke, "The Great Powers," [1833], in ibid., pp. 142–43.

28. Jules Michelet, *History of the French Revolution,* trans. Charles Cocks, ed. Gordon Wright (Chicago, 1967), pp. 3, 13.

29. Ibid., p. 449.

30. Jules Michelet, *The People,* trans. John P. McKay (Urbana, Ill., 1973), p. 9.

31. Ibid., pp. 19, 183, 188, 199.

CHAPTER 4

1. Carlton J. H. Hayes, "Nationalism as a Religion," in Hayes, *Essays on Nationalism* (New York, 1966), pp. 93–125; quotations on pp. 95–96.

2. For examples of recent work on the overlapping themes of nationalism and religion, see Conor Cruise O'Brien, *God Land: Reflections on Religion and Nationalism* (Cambridge, Mass., 1988) and the essays in *Many Are Chosen: Divine Election and Western Nationalism,* ed. William R. Hutchison and Hartmut Lehmann (Minneapolis, 1994).

3. Michelet, *The People*, pp. 180–81.

4. Mazzini, *The Duties of Man*, p. 29. The quotation comes from a section in *Duties* entitled "God," which was first published in 1844.

5. For discussion of the Protestant national feeling in Britain, see Greenfeld, *Nationalism*, pp. 53–66; and Colley, *Britons*, pp. 11–54. On Protestantism and American nationalism, see O'Brien, *God Land*, pp. 52–63; James H. Moorhead, "The American Israel: Protestant Tribalism and Universal Mission," in Hutchison and Lehmann, eds., *Many Are Chosen*, pp. 145–166; and Ernest Lee Tuveson, *Redeemer Nation: The Idea of America's Millennial Role* (Chicago, 1968).

6. Friedrich Schleiermacher to Baron von Stein, 24 November 1809 [?], quoted in Kohn, *Prelude to Nation-States*, p. 249.

7. Mickiewicz, *Les Slaves*, pp. 49, 120.

8. Mazzini, *Duties of Man*, pp. 54–56.

9. Ibid., pp. 58–59.

10. Adam Mickiewicz, *The Books of the Polish Nation and Pilgrims* [1832], in *Poems by Adam Mickiewicz*, ed. and trans. George R. Noyes, (New York, 1944), p. 380.

11. Mazzini, *Duties of Man*, p. 57.

12. Johann Draseke, *Vaterlandsfreude: Eine Dankpredigt zur Feier des Tages von Leipzig* (1815), p. 24; quoted in Hoover, *Gospel of Nationalism*, p. 73.

13. Hayes, "Nationalism as a Religion," pp. 104–25. Hayes sometimes suggested that nationalism had replaced traditional religion, but he also referred to the intersection of nationalist and religious practices as a "syncretism." See also Salo Wittmayer Baron, *Modern Nationalism and Religion* (New York, 1947).

14. Fichte, *Addresses*, pp. 95–96.

15. Mazzini, "Faith and the Future," in Mazzini, *Duties of Man*, p. 183; Mazzini wrote this essay in 1835.

16. For more on the role of national monuments in nationalist ideologies, see Mosse, *Nationalization of the Masses* (New York, 1975), pp. 47–72, and Adam J. Lerner, "The Nineteenth-Century Monument and the Embodiment of National Time," in Ringrose and Lerner, eds., *Reimagining the Nation*, pp. 176–96.

17. Abraham Keteltas, *God Arising and Pleading His People's Cause . . .* , *a sermon preached October 5, 1777 in . . . Newburyport* (1777), in Winthrop S. Hudson, ed., *Nationalism and Religion in America: Concepts of American Identity and Mission* (New York, 1970), pp. 49, 52–53.

18. Ernst Moritz Arndt, *Geist der Zeit*, part three [1813], quoted in Kohn, *Prelude to Nation-States*, p. 261.

19. Fichte, *Addresses*, p. 136.

20. Ibid., p. 142.

21. Mazzini, *Duties of Man*, p. 55.

22. Quoted passages from "The Marsaillaise" are from the translation in *The New Encyclopaedia Britannica*, 15th ed., vol. 7 (Chicago, 1993), p. 875. For a more detailed account of the military themes in national anthems, see George L. Mosse's essay "National Anthems: The Nation Militant," in his book *Confronting the Nation: Jewish and Western Nationalism* (Hanover, N.H., 1993), pp. 13–26. On the theme of sacrifice and nationalist thought, see Jean Bethke Elshtain, "Sovereignty, Identity, Sacrifice," in Ringrose and Lerner, eds., *Reimagining the Nation*, pp. 159–175.

CHAPTER 5

1. For examples of such antiessentialist views, see the following essays in *Becoming National*, ed. Geoff Eley and Ronald Grigor Suny (New York and Oxford, 1996): Anne McClintock, " 'No Longer in a Future Heaven': Nationalism, Gender, and Race," pp. 260–84; Stuart Hall, "Ethnicity: Identity and Difference," pp. 339–49; and Paul Gilroy, "One Nation under a Groove: The Cultural Politics of 'Race' and Racism in Britain," pp. 352–69.

2. Colley, *Britons*, p. 252.

3. Agulhon, *Marianne into Battle*, p. 129.

4. Michael D. Biddiss, ed., *Gobineau: Selected Political Writings* (New York, 1970), p. 89. This passage comes from Gobineau's *Essay on the Inequality of the Human Races* (1853–1855).

5. Ralph Waldo Emerson, *The Collected Works of Ralph Waldo Emerson*, vol. 5, *English Traits*, historical intro. Philip Nicoloff, notes Robert E. Burkholder, and textual intro. Douglas Emery Wilson (Cambridge, Mass., 1994), pp. 36–37, 132. *English Traits* was first published in 1856.

6. Joseph Mazzini, *Duties of Man*, pp. 54–55. The quotation comes from a chapter entitled "Duties to Country," which Mazzini first published in 1858.

7. George L. Mosse, *Nationalism and Sexuality: Middle-Class Morality and Sexual Norms in Modern Europe* (Madison, 1985), pp. 9, 13, 64, 98. For more on the fusion of ideas about gender, sexual behavior, and nations, see the essays in *Nationalisms and Sexualities*, ed. Andrew Parker, Mary Russo, Doris Sommer, and Patricia Yaeger, (New York, 1992).

8. Mickiewicz, *Les Slaves*, p. 338.

9. Ibid.

10. Mazzini, *Duties of Man*, p. 61.

11. Michelet, *The People*, pp. 57, 167.

12. Mazzini, *Duties of Man*, p. 61.

13. Fichte, *Addresses*, pp. 132, 142. Fichte himself had one son, who also became a philosopher.

14. Michelet, *The People,* pp. 120, 209.

15. Mazzini, *Duties of Man,* pp. 61–62, 65–66. All these passages appeared in a chapter called "Duties to the Family," which was first published in 1858. For an excellent analysis of how families shape the national identities of individuals, see Etienne Balibar, "The Nation Form: History and Ideology," in Eley and Suny, eds., *Becoming National,* pp. 132–49.

16. George Mosse describes the nationalist anxiety about "nonproductive" sexual behavior in *Nationalism and Sexuality,* pp. 23–40.

17. Michelet, *The People,* p. 168. For information on the enduring French anxiety about birth rates, see Karen Offen, "Depopulation, Nationalism, and Feminism in Fin-de-Siècle France," *American Historical Review* 89 (1984):648–76.

18. For more on "captivity narratives" and early American national identity, see Carroll Smith-Rosenberg, "Captured Subjects/Savage Others: Violently Engendering the New American," *Gender and History* 5 (1993):177–95, and Kathryn Zabelle Derounian-Stodola and James Arthur Levernier, *The Indian Captivity Narrative, 1550–1900* (New York, 1993).

19. See the discussion of French anxiety about sexual assaults from German soldiers in Ouriel Reshef, *Guerre, Mythes et Caricature: au berceau d'une mentalité française* (Paris, 1984), pp. 37–87, 153–207; on the French view of German sexual threats at the time of World War I, see Ruth Harris, "The 'Child of the Barbarian': Rape, Race, and Nationalism in France during the First World War," *Past and Present* 141 (1993):170–206.

20. Fichte, *Addresses,* pp. 52, 65, 68, 72, 125–26.

21. Meinecke, *Cosmopolitanism,* p. 9.

22. Alfred Rosenberg, *The Myth of the Twentieth Century,* excerpt in Louis L. Snyder, *The Idea of Racialism, Its Meaning and History* (Princeton, 1962), p. 158.

23. Robert Knox, *The Races of Men: A Fragment* (Philadelphia, 1850; reprint, Miami, 1969), pp. 43, 46, 48, 221.

24. Ibid., p. 49.

25. Emerson, *English Traits,* pp. 24–28, 75–76, 155, 177.

26. George Bancroft, *History of the United States,* 10th ed., vol. 1 (Boston, 1844), pp. 180–82; 12th ed., vol. 2 (Boston, 1845), p. 452.

27. Ibid., 12th ed., vol. 3 (Boston, 1846), p. 302.

28. Biddiss, ed., *Gobineau: Political Writings,* p. 59.

29. Ibid., pp. 65, 68; see also pp. 90, 162.

30. Ibid., pp. 136–40 (first quotation on p. 140), 172–73.

31. Fichte, *Addresses,* pp. 268–69.

32. Michelet, *The People,* pp. 192–93, 209.

33. Ibid., p. 210.

34. Albert J. Beveridge, "On the Mission of the American Race," speech in the United States Senate, 9 January 1900, excerpt in Snyder, *Idea of Racialism*, p. 168.

CHAPTER 6

1. For historical analysis of the religious themes in American nationalism, see Tuveson, *Redeemer Nation;* O'Brien, *God Land;* Paul C. Nagel, *This Sacred Trust: American Nationality, 1798–1898* (Oxford and New York, 1971); and the early American texts in Hudson, ed., *Nationalism and Religion in America.* On the enduring conception of American uniqueness, see Seymour Martin Lipset, *American Exceptionalism: A Double-Edged Sword* (New York, 1996).

2. John Louis Sullivan, "The Great Nation of Futurity," in *The United States Magazine and Democratic Review* (November 1839), quoted in Hans Kohn, *American Nationalism: An Interpretative Essay* (New York, 1957), p. 153.

3. Herman Melville, *White-Jacket, or The World in a Man-of-War,* ed. A. R. Humphreys (Oxford, 1966), p. 158.

4. Richard M. Johnson, Speech in Congress, 11 December 1811, in Rebecca Brooks Gruver, *American Nationalism, 1783–1830: A Self-Portrait* (New York, 1970), p. 205. This book provides an excellent, edited collection of early American texts.

5. Richmond *Enquirer,* 22 February 1815, in ibid., p. 224.

6. Timothy Flint, *Indian Wars of the West* (1833), in ibid., pp. 151–52.

7. For more information on Freneau's life and work, see Mary Weatherspoon Bowden, *Philip Freneau* (Boston, 1976), and Lewis Leary, *That Rascal Freneau: A Study in Literary Failure* (New York, 1964).

8. Philip Freneau, "To his Excellency George Washington" [September 1781], in Hiltner, ed., *Newspaper Verse,* p. 83.

9. Philip Freneau, "Stanzas, Occasioned by the Death of General George Washington" [January 1800], in ibid., p. 629.

10. Ibid., p. 630. Freneau's praise for other "Founding Fathers" appears in "Stanzas, Occasioned by the Death of Dr. Franklin" [April 1790], and in "Lines Addressed to Mr. Jefferson, on his approaching retirement from the presidency of the United States" [March 1809], both in ibid., pp. 387, 662–65.

11. Philip Freneau, "Lines occasioned by reading Mr. Paine's RIGHTS OF MAN" [May 1791], in ibid., p. 457. The prose quotations are from Freneau's article "Women's Influence on Men and Politics—The Importance of Free Opinion," *National Gazette,* 26 December 1792, in Marsh, ed., *Prose of Freneau,* pp. 293–94.

12. Philip Freneau, "Independence" [July 1792], in Hiltner, ed., *Newspaper Verse,* p. 497.

13. Philip Freneau, "Stanzas on the Emmigration to America, and peopling the Western Country" [1785], in ibid., p. 230.

14. Philip Freneau, "The Republic and Liberty" [June 1798], in ibid., p. 618.

15. Philip Freneau, ["The Greatness of America"], *The Miscellaneous Works of Philip Freneau* (1788), in Marsh, ed., *Prose of Freneau,* pp. 227–28.

16. Philip Freneau, "On the American and French Revolutions" [March 1790], in Hiltner, ed., *Newspaper Verse,* p. 368.

17. Philip Freneau, "To the Memory of the brave, accomplished and patriotic Col. JOHN LAURENS" [October 1787], in ibid., p. 311; earlier quotation, p. 653; see also "To the memory of the brave Americans . . . who fell in the action of September 8, 1781" [1786], and "Reflections, on walking . . . where many Americans were interred from the Prison Ships . . ." [April 1803], both in ibid., pp. 96, 653..

18. Philip Freneau, "The Infamy of Kings—and the Virtue of American Farmers," *Letters on Various Interesting and Important Subjects* (1799), in Marsh, ed., *Prose of Freneau,* pp. 401–02; see also Freneau, ["Royal Dangers in the American Stage"], *National Gazette,* 6 March 1793, in ibid., pp. 295–96.

19. Philip Freneau, "Reflections on my Journey from the Tallassee Towns to the settlements on the river Hudson. By OPAY MICO . . . ," New York *Daily Advertiser,* 31 August 1790, in ibid., pp. 256–57.

20. Philip Freneau, "Description of NEW YORK one-hundred and fifty years hence . . . ," New York *Daily Advertiser,* 12 and 14 June 1790, in ibid., pp.240–43.

21. For more information on Bancroft's life and work, see Russel B. Nye, *George Bancroft* (New York, 1964), and Lilian Handlin, *George Bancroft: The Intellectual as Democrat* (New York, 1984).

22. George Bancroft, *History of the United States, From the Discovery of the American Continent,* vol. 7 (Boston, 1858), p. 400.

23. Bancroft, *History,* vol. 4 (Boston, 1852), p. 13.

24. Ibid., p. 12.

25. Ibid., vol. 1 (Boston, 1834), pp. 1, 3.

26. Ibid., vol. 7, pp. 22–23.

27. Ibid., vol. 1, pp. 2–3; also, vol. 8 (Boston, 1860), p. 473, and vol. 10 (Boston, 1874), p. 592.

28. Ibid., vol. 1, p. 4; also, vol. 5 (Boston, 1854), pp. 4–5, 30–31, 320; vol. 4, p. 154; and vol. 7, p. 21. See also George Bancroft, *Literary and Historical Miscellanies* (New York, 1855), pp. 424–25.

29. Bancroft, *History,* vol. 7, pp. 295–96.

30. Ibid., pp. 290–91.

31. Ibid., p. 55.

32. Ibid., vol. 3, pp. 406, 408.

33. Ibid., vol. 4, pp. 456–57.

34. This Memorial Address appeared in numerous editions; see, for example, George Bancroft, *Abraham Lincoln: A Tribute* (New York, 1908), pp. 25, 66–69.

35. Abraham Lincoln, *The Collected Works of Abraham Lincoln*, vol. 7, ed. Roy P. Basler, Marion Dolores Pratt, and Lloyd A. Dunlap (New Brunswick, N.J., 1953), p. 23.

Bibliographic Essay

The literature on nationalism deals with all regions of the world, analyzes events over several centuries, and ranges widely in approach—from the highly theoretical to the quantitative, from the political to the cultural or economic. Most recent scholars have been skeptical about the claims and consequences of nationalist thought, but few would deny that nationalism has also provided important and even liberating affirmations of group identity, freedom, and human rights. Debates about "good" and "bad" nationalisms therefore continue to evolve among analysts of nationalism throughout the world.

These continuing debates draw on the many interpretations that earlier authors have already developed, and the arguments often return to themes that have been discussed in this book. In order to understand the history of such debates, it is still helpful to read the classic work by Hans Kohn, *The Idea of Nationalism: A Study in its Origins and Background* (New York: Macmillan, 1944). Kohn discusses the intellectual origins of nationalist thought from antiquity down to the early nineteenth century. Other influential early studies of nationalist ideas include Carlton J. H. Hayes, *Essays on Nationalism* (New York: Russell & Russell, 1926, rept., 1966), and Ernest Renan, "What Is a Nation?" (1882), both of which seek to explain how and why people identify with a nation. Renan's essay can be found in Goeff Eley and Ronald Grigor Suny, eds., *Becoming National: A Reader* (New York: Oxford University Press, 1996), which is an outstanding compilation of influential essays on nationalist theories and identities. The influence of contemporary cultural studies can be seen in many of these essays, but for other examples of this cultural approach, see Stuart Hall and Paul du Gay, eds., *Questions of Cultural Identity* (London: Sage, 1996).

The theoretical starting point for much of the recent writing on nationalism derives from Benedict Anderson's paradigm-shaping *Imagined Communities: Reflections on the Origin and Spread of Nationalism* (London: Verso, 2d ed., 1991). See also the important work of Ernest Gellner, *Nations and Nationalism* (Ithaca: Cornell University Press, 1983), which analyzes the economic component of nationalist institutions, and the collection of Eric Hobsbawm and Terrence Ranger, eds., *The Invention of Tradition* (Cambridge: Cambridge University Press, 1983), which provides examples of how various national cultures have constructed images of their past. Hobsbawm also explores economic influences on nationalism in his book *Nations and Nationalism since 1780: Programme, myth, reality* (Cambridge: Cambridge University Press, 1990), whereas John Breuilly stresses nationalism's political dimensions in *Nationalism and the State* (Chicago: University of Chicago Press, 1982). Other useful surveys of nationalist movements can be found in Peter Alter, *Nationalism* (London: Edward Arnold, 2d ed., 1994), in Hugh Seton-Watson, *Nations and States: An Enquiry into the Origins of Nations and the Politics of Nationalism* (Boulder: Westview Press, 1977), and in Liah Greenfeld, *Nationalism: Five Roads to Modernity* (Cambridge: Harvard University Press, 1992).

Greenfeld's work stresses the contrasts between "Western" (individualist) and "Eastern" (collectivist) nationalist cultures, thus adding to the view of different nationalisms that appears in Rogers Brubaker's *Citizenship and Nationhood in France and Germany* (Cambridge: Harvard University Press, 1992). The relation between these two important European nationalisms is also explored with insight in Louis Dumont, *German Ideology: From France to Germany and Back* (Chicago: University of Chicago Press, 1994). A more general account of various kinds of nationalist thought appears in the comprehensive work of Anthony D. Smith, *Theories of Nationalism* (New York: Holmes and Meier, 2d ed., 1983). For an important critique of the Western orientation in most theoretical studies of nationalism, see two books by Partha Chatterjee, *Nationalist Thought and the Colonial World—A Derivative Discourse?* (London: Zed Books, 1986) and *The Nation and its Fragments: Studies in Colonial and Post-Colonial Histories* (Princeton: Princeton University Press, 1993). A useful, well-organized collection of nationalist writings from both Western and non-Western cultures is available in Omar Dahbour and Micheline R. Ishay, eds., *The Nationalism Reader* (Atlantic Highlands, N.J.: Humanities Press, 1995).

There is a huge literature on the American and French Revolutions, but for introductions to the new national themes in these political events see Gordon S. Wood, *The Radicalism of the American Revolution* (New York: Alfred A. Knopf, 1992), and Lynn Hunt, *Politics, Culture, and Class in the French Revolution* (Berkeley: University of California Press, 1984). Other useful studies of nationalism during this formative era include Hans Kohn, *Prelude to Nation-States: The French and German Experience, 1789–1815* (Princeton: D. Van Nostrand, 1967), the essays in Otto Dann and John Dinwiddy, eds., *Nationalism in the Age of the French Revolution* (London: Hambledon Press, 1988), and the more specialized study by William H. Sewell Jr., *A Rhetoric of Bourgeois Revolution: The Abbé Sieyès and "What Is the Third Estate?"* (Durham: Duke University Press, 1994). The new French political culture is also discussed with insight in Brian Jenkins, *Nationalism in France: Class and Nation since 1789* (London: Routledge, 1990). On the military *esprit* of the new national armies, see John A. Lynn, *The Bayonets of the Republic: Motivation and Tactics in the Army of Revolutionary France, 1791–94* (Urbana: University of Illinois Press, 1984), and Alan Forrest, *Soldiers of the French Revolution* (Durham: Duke University Press, 1990).

The wider political and cultural influences of revolutionary events are discussed in the classic work by R. R. Palmer, *The Age of the Democratic Revolution*, 2 vols. (Princeton: Princeton University Press, 1959, 1964). Valuable studies of the new nationalisms in the anti-French political cultures of the era are available in Hagen Schulze, *The Course of German Nationalism, From Frederick the Great to Bismarck, 1763–1867* (Cambridge: Cambridge University Press, 1991), Eugene Newton Anderson, *Nationalism and the Cultural Crisis in Prussia, 1806–1815* (New York: Octagon Books, 1966), and Linda Colley, *Britons: Forging the Nation, 1707–1837* (New Haven: Yale University Press, 1992).

Important examples of the new literary interest in how nations emerge through "writing" appear in the influential work of Homi Bhabha, ed., *Nation and Narration* (London: Routledge, 1990). Bhabha and the other contributors to this book often draw on poststructuralist literary theories to deconstruct the imagined unity of national narratives—a method that can be found also in Bhabha's *The Location of Culture* (London: Routledge, 1994). For more traditional studies of the role of writing and intellectuals in nationalism (e.g., Fichte), see the criticisms in Elie Kedourie, *Nationalism* (London: Blackwell, 4th ed., 1993), and the equally hostile account of "messianic" nationalists (e.g., Michelet, Mickiewicz, Mazzini) in Jacob Talmon, *Political Messianism: The Romantic Phase* (London: Secker and Warburg, 1960). The influence of intellectuals in early-nineteenth-century Western European national cultures is also analyzed in Martin Thom, *Republics, Nations, and Tribes* (London: Verso,

1995), and there is an informative study of Polish nationalist intellectuals in Andrzej Walicki, *Philosophy and Romantic Nationalism: The Case of Poland* (Oxford: Clarendon Press, 1982).

Contemporary historians have given increasing attention to the cultural institutions in which nationalist ideas and memories are represented and conveyed to national populations through symbols, languages, and rituals. See, for example, George Mosse, *The Nationalization of the Masses: Political Symbolism and Mass Movements in Germany from the Napoleonic Wars through the Third Reich* (New York: Howard Fertig, 1975); John R. Gillis, ed., *Commemorations: The Politics of National Identity* (Princeton: Princeton University Press, 1994); Maurice Agulhon, *Marianne into Battle: Republican Imagery and Symbolism in France, 1789–1880* (Cambridge: Cambridge University Press, 1981); and Marjorie Ringrose and Adam J. Lerner, eds., *Reimagining the Nation* (Buckingham: Open University Press, 1993). The modern communicative networks that spread nationalist thought have been analyzed in a classic study by Karl W. Deutsch called *Nationalism and Social Communication: An Inquiry into the Foundations of Nationality* (Cambridge: MIT Press; New York: Wiley, 1953). A more specialized study of linguistic nationalism can be found in Michael Townson, *Mother-Tongue and Fatherland: Language and Politics in German* (Manchester: Manchester University Press, 1992).

The connections between religion and nationalism became an important theme in the early essays of Carlton J. H. Hayes (noted earlier) and in Hayes's later book, *Nationalism: A Religion* (New York: Macmillan, 1960). Other important works on this theme include the detailed study by Salo Wittmayer Baron, *Modern Nationalism and Religion* (New York: Harper and Brothers, 1947), the wide-ranging essays in William R. Hutchison and Hartmut Lehmann, eds., *Many are Chosen: Divine Election and Western Nationalism* (Minneapolis: Fortress Press, 1994), and the provocative commentary by Conor Cruise O'Brien, *God Land: Reflections on Religion and Nationalism* (Cambridge: Harvard University Press, 1988). The enduring influence of religious themes in American nationalism has been examined in Ernest Lee Tuveson, *Redeemer Nation: The Idea of America's Millennial Role* (Chicago: University of Chicago Press, 1968); and Winthrop S. Hudson has collected an excellent group of documents on this theme in *Nationalism and Religion in America: Concepts of American Identity and Mission* (New York: Harper and Row, 1970).

A growing literature on the complex links between nationalism, gender roles, and sexuality owes much to the insights of George Mosse in *Nationalism and Sexuality: Middle-Class Morality and Sexual Norms in Modern Europe* (Madison: University of Wisconsin Press, 1985). Mosse's themes have been explored and expanded by other authors in Andrew Parker, Mary Russo, Doris Sommer, and Patricia Yaeger, eds., *Nation-*

alisms and Sexualities (New York: Routledge, 1992). See also the analysis of gender ideologies in Anne McClintock, *Imperial Leather: Race, Gender and Sexuality in the Colonial Contest* (New York: Routledge, 1995), and in the special issue of the journal *Gender and History* 5 (Summer 1993) on "Gender, Nationalisms, and National Identities."

Many of the general histories of nationalism note the influence of racial theories, but for other commentaries on this theme see the analysis and documents in Louis L. Snyder, *The Idea of Racialism: Its Meaning and History* (Princeton: D. Van Nostrand, 1962), and the informative study by Michael D. Biddiss titled *Father of Racist Ideology: The Social and Political Thought of Count Gobineau* (London: Weidenfeld and Nicolson, 1970). Although "ethnicity" does not have the same meanings as "race," this concept has often been linked to racial theories and remains important for nationalisms today. See, for example, Anthony D. Smith, *The Ethnic Origins of Nations* (Oxford: Blackwell, 1986).

The legacy of racialized cultural assumptions is also examined by various authors in Homi Bhabha's edited collection, *Nation and Narration* (noted earlier), in Patrick Williams and Laura Chrisman, eds., *Colonial Discourse and Post-Colonial Theory: A Reader* (New York: Harvester Wheatsheaf, 1993), and with special attention to the African Diaspora, in the important work of Paul Gilroy, *The Black Atlantic: Modernity and Double Consciousness* (Cambridge: Harvard University Press, 1993).

Like other nationalisms, American nationalism has been influenced by anxieties about race, immigration, and ethnicity (the works of Bhabha and Gilroy note some of these issues), and religious themes have been prominent in many strands of American exceptionalism (as the works on nationalism and religion suggest). For studies of these and other themes in American nationalism, see Hans Kohn, *American Nationalism: An Interpretative Essay* (New York: Macmillan, 1957), Paul C. Nagel, *This Sacred Trust: American Nationality, 1798–1898* (New York: Oxford University Press, 1971), and Seymour Martin Lipset, *American Exceptionalism: A Double-Edged Sword* (New York: Norton, 1996). An outstanding collection of documents from early American national culture can be found in Rebecca Brooks Gruver, *American Nationalism, 1783–1830: A Self-Portrait* (New York: G. P. Putnam's Sons, 1970). On the specific issue of American racial ideologies, see Reginald Horsman, *Race and Manifest Destiny: The Origins of American Racial Anglo-Saxonism* (Cambridge, Mass.: Harvard University Press, 1981).

For insightful introductions to the early and continuing construction of America's national memory and identity, see two books by Michael Kammen, *A Season of Youth: The American Revolution and the Historical Imagination* (New York: Alfred A. Knopf, 1978) and *Mystic Chords of Memory: The Transformation of Tradition in American Culture* (New York: Alfred

A. Knopf, 1991); on this same issue, see Wilbur Zelinsky, *Nation into State: The Shifting Symbolic Foundations of American Nationalism* (Chapel Hill: University of North Carolina Press, 1988). Finally, the history of America's remembrances of national texts and events can be explored through another work by Michael Kammen, *A Machine That Would Go of Itself: The Constitution in American Culture* (New York: Alfred A. Knopf, 1986), and in the recent works of Len Travers, *Celebrating the Fourth: Independence Day and the Rites of Nationalism in the Early Republic* (Amherst: University of Massachusetts Press, 1997), and Pauline Maier, *American Scripture: Making the Declaration of Independence* (New York: Alfred A. Knopf, 1997).

Index

The Author

Lloyd Kramer is professor of history at the University of North Carolina, Chapel Hill. He is the author of *Threshold of a New World: Intellectuals and the Exile Experience in Paris, 1830–1848* (1988) and *Lafayette in Two Worlds: Public Cultures and Personal Identities in an Age of Revolutions* (1996). He is also coeditor of *Learning History in America: Schools, Cultures, and Politics* (1994).

The Editor

Michael S. Roth is the assistant director of the Scholars and Seminars program at the Getty Research Institute in Los Angeles. Previously, he was professor of history and cultural studies at Scripps College and the Claremont Graduate School. His books include *Psychoanalysis as History: Negation and Freedom in Freud* (1987, 1995), *Knowing and History: Appropriations of Hegel in Twentieth Century France* (1988), and *The Ironist's Cage: Memory, Trauma, and the Construction of History* (1995).